Keepers of the Flame

Keepers of the Flame

by JANET PETERSON
and LaRENE GAUNT

Deseret Book Company
Salt Lake City, Utah

Photographs on pages 2, 18, 32, 50, 66, 98, 136, and 158 courtesy Museum of Church History and Art. Photograph on page 118 © LDS Church. Used by permission.

Library of Congress Cataloging-in-Publication Data

Peterson, Janet, 1946–
    Keepers of the flame: Presidents of the Young Women / Janet Peterson, LaRene Gaunt.
       p. cm.
    Includes index.
    ISBN 0-87579-670-2
    1. Young Women (Church of Jesus Christ of Latter-day Saints) —
Biography.   2. Women, Mormon — Biography.   I. Gaunt, LaRene.
II. Title.
BX8693.G38   1993
267′.449332′0922 — dc20
[B]   92-40148
                                                      CIP

Printed in the United States of America

10   9   8   7   6   5   4   3   2   1

*To the Young Women—especially those
of the Salt Lake Brighton Stake
and the Willow Canyon Eighth Ward—
future keepers of the flame*

Contents

Preface

*T*he Young Gentlemen and Ladies' Relief Society of Nauvoo, the first organization in The Church of Jesus Christ of Latter-day Saints for young people, was an outgrowth of the Female Relief Society of Nauvoo, organized in 1842, and was the predecessor of the Young Ladies' Retrenchment Association.

In January 1843, a group of young men and women gathered at the home of Heber C. Kimball, a member of the Quorum of the Twelve Apostles, in Nauvoo, Illinois. According to the *Times and Seasons,* during the course of their conversation the young people lamented "the loose style of their morals — the frivolous manner in which they spent their time — and their too frequent attendance at balls, parties, etc."[1] Elder Kimball suggested that a more formal meeting of "young ladies and gentlemen" be called so that he could instruct them. At that meeting, which was held at the house of a Brother Billings, Elder Kimball talked about the duties of children to their parents and exhorted the youths to "lay aside their vanity, light-mindedness, pride, and frivolity; and endeavor to show themselves worthy of the religion which they had embraced; advising them to shun evil company . . . and to be obedient to their parents."[2]

The group voted to meet again the following week. When a schoolroom proved to be too small for the gathering, they moved to the home of Joseph Smith, which also proved to be inadequate for the number who wanted to attend.

The next meeting was held in the same room over the

Prophet's store where the Relief Society had been organized in March 1842. The Prophet himself attended the next meeting and addressed the youth. He thanked Elder Kimball for beginning "the good and glorious work" and said, according to one account, that " 'when gray hairs should his [Joseph's] temples adorn,' he could look back with pleasure upon the winter of 1843, when he was engaged in promoting the cause of benevolence, and preparing his young friends for the glorious career which awaited them."[3] He expressed his hope that such meetings would continue and that the young people would follow his teachings.

The gatherings, which became known as the Young People's meetings, continued through February and March. On March 21, the group elected officers and adopted resolutions that began as follows:

"Whereas, The young gentlemen and ladies, citizens of the city of Nauvoo, are desirous of aiding and ameliorating the condition of the poor and of carrying out the principles of charity and benevolence, as taught in the holy Scriptures, therefore, be it resolved, That we form ourselves into a society to be styled the 'Young Gentlemen and Ladies' Relief Society of Nauvoo,' and that we be governed by the following articles. . . . "[4]

One article called for "a committee of vigilance, consisting of five persons, whose duties it shall be to search out the poor of our city, and make known to the society the wants of those whom they, in their judgment, shall consider most deserving of our assistance."[5] Other articles established meetings on the last Tuesday of each month, outlined the election and duties of the officers, and set criteria for admittance: a candidate had to be under thirty years of age and of "good moral character." Elders Jedediah M. Grant, Brigham Young, and Heber C. Kimball addressed subsequent meetings.

Joseph Smith did not live to see gray hairs adorn his temples, for he was martyred the following year, on June 27, 1844. Because of increased anti-Mormon sentiment and persecution following the martyrdom, the Saints were forced to leave Nauvoo and to seek refuge in the Great Salt Lake Valley.

More than twenty years later and in another setting some fourteen hundred miles from Nauvoo, the young ladies and gentlemen were again organized, but this time separately. On November 28, 1869, a Sunday evening, President Brigham Young rang the prayer bell to call the women in his family, both young and old, to a meeting in the front parlor of the Lion House. Also invited were President George A. Smith, a counselor in the First Presidency, and his wife, Bathsheba. Following the evening prayer, Brigham told his family:

"All Israel are looking to my family and watching the example set by my wives and children. For this reason I desire to organize my own family first into a society for the promotion of habits of order, thrift, industry, and charity; and above all things I desire them to retrench from their extravagance in dress, in eating and even in speech. The time has come when the sisters must agree to give up their follies of dress and cultivate a modest apparel, a meek deportment, and to set an example worthy of imitation before the people of the world. I am weary of the manner in which our women seek to outdo each other in all the foolish fashions of the world. . . .

"I have long had it in my mind to organize the young ladies of Zion into an association so that they might assist the older members of the Church, their fathers and mothers, in propagating, teaching, and practicing the principles I have been so long teaching. There is need for the young daughters of Israel to get a living testimony of the truth. . . . For this purpose I desire to establish this organization and want my family to lead out in the great work. We are about to organize a retrenchment Association, which I want you all to join, and I want you to vote to retrench in your dress, in your tables, in your speech, wherein you have been guilty of silly, extravagant speeches and light-mindedness of thought. Retrench in everything that is not good and beautiful, not to make yourselves unhappy, but to live so that you may be truly happy in this life and the life to come."[6]

President Young called upon his wives to express their feelings and asked all present to vote to sustain his proposal to organize his daughters into a retrenchment association. The voting was unanimous. President George A. Smith then testified that Brigham had spoken as a prophet.

President Young asked Eliza R. Snow, one of his wives and the general president of the Relief Society, to assist in organizing the new association. Articles were drawn up, officers were elected, and a name was suggested — the Young Ladies' Department of the Cooperative Retrenchment Association, which was soon shortened to the Young Ladies' Retrenchment Association. Ella Young Empey was elected president, and her sisters Emily Young Clawson, Zina Young Williams, Maria Young Dougall, Caroline Young, Dora Young, and Phebe Young were named as her counselors. Sister Snow wrote the resolutions adopted by the new organization: "Resolved, that realizing ourselves to be . . . daughters of apostles, prophets, and elders of Israel, and, as such, that high responsibilities rest upon us, and that we shall be held accountable to God not only for the privileges we inherit from our fathers, but also for the blessings we enjoy as Latter-day Saints, we feel to unite and . . . uphold and sustain each other in doing good."[7]

The new Retrenchment Association met regularly that winter. The first ward association was organized in the Nineteenth Ward in Salt Lake City in 1870 after Lona Pratt, a daughter of Parley P. Pratt and a friend of Dora Young, had heard Dora's enthusiastic reports of the new organization and wanted to have a similar one for her friends. At Lona's invitation, a group of young women met at a schoolhouse where she taught and formed an association.

Within a year, scores of Retrenchment Associations were organized in Salt Lake City, Ogden, Provo, Logan, Brigham City, Bountiful, and other communities, usually under the direction of Eliza R. Snow. The association was divided into junior and senior programs, with Sister Snow and Zina D. H. Young, her counselor in the Relief Society, directing the younger girls and Mary Isabella Horne directing the older ones. Each organization was independent because there was not a general presidency nor approved guidelines, but most of them followed the resolutions of the original group.

A similar association for the young men, the Young Men's Mutual Improvement Association, was organized in 1875. Two years later the Retrenchment Society adopted a companion name and became known as the Young Ladies' National Mutual Improvement Association (known as the YLMIA).

The first stake YLMIA board was organized in 1878 in the

Salt Lake Stake, which covered a large part of the Salt Lake Valley. On June 19, 1880, under the direction of President John Taylor, the first general presidency of the Young Ladies' National Mutual Improvement Association was organized, with Elmina Shepard Taylor as president and Margaret Young Taylor and Martha Horne as counselors. Elmina Taylor served for twenty-four years, until her death in 1904.

Nine other general presidents, "keepers of the flame," have served the young women of the Church:
- Martha Horne Tingey, 1904–29
- Ruth May Fox, 1929–37
- Lucy Grant Cannon, 1937–48
- Bertha Stone Reeder, 1948–61
- Florence Smith Jacobsen, 1961–72
- Ruth Hardy Funk, 1972–78
- Elaine Cannon, 1978–84
- Ardeth Greene Kapp, 1984–92
- Janette Callister Hales, 1992–

From the time Brigham Young organized the Young Ladies' Department of the Cooperative Retrenchment Association for his daughters in 1869 to more than a century later when the present name, the Young Women, was designated, the young women's auxiliary has undergone several name changes:
- 1877, Young Ladies' National Mutual Improvement Association
- 1904, Young Ladies' Mutual Improvement Association
- 1934, Young Women's Mutual Improvement Association
- 1972, Aaronic Priesthood Mutual Improvement Association (Young Women)
- 1974, Young Women

The current Young Women program grew from the desires of young women to improve themselves, to develop their talents, to serve others, and to strengthen their testimonies of Jesus Christ. A study of the lives of the ten women who have led the young women of the Church since 1880 reveals how each of these leaders has implemented the original goals into programs for her particular day and how each, working through inspiration from the Lord and often at great personal sacrifice, has helped build his kingdom by serving the young women of Zion.

Acknowledgments

We wish to thank Eleanor Knowles, our editor at Deseret Book Company, for again helping us develop an idea into a manuscript and for polishing it with insight and skill; the staff of the Church Historical Library and Church Archives for helping us with our research; Calvin R. Stephens for reading the manuscript and offering his historical expertise; and Carolyn J. Rasmus, administrative assistant to Ardeth G. Kapp and Janette C. Hales, for generously sharing her time and her vision of Young Women.

Families of the presidents, counselors in the general presidencies, secretaries and general board members have freely given us their materials and perspectives and have made valuable suggestions. We especially thank Burton S. Tingey, Joseph Tingey, Emily Wright, Mary Ellen Elggren, George I. Cannon, Jean Cannon Willis, Stanley Cannon, Grant C Aadnesen, Oertel Aadnesen Hoit, Theodore M. Jacobsen, Allyson Funk Gurney, Nancy Funk Pulsipher, Jenny Jo Funk Emery, Marcus C. Funk, D. James Cannon, James Q. Cannon, Tony Cannon, Carla Cannon, Marion D. Hanks, Winnifred C. Jardine, Heber B. Kapp, Shirley Greene Burnham, Sharon Greene Larsen, Shelly Larsen, Ann Hales Nevers, Jane Hales Ricks, Thomas C. Hales, Karen Hales Parkinson, and Mary Hales.

Most of all, we thank our families for their patient and loving support: our husbands, Larry Peterson and David Gaunt; and our children, Scott, Stephanie, Tom, Greg, Jeffrey, and Brent Peterson; and Angela, Dennis, and Lisa Gaunt.

Keepers of the Flame

1

Elmina Shepard Taylor
1880–1904

At the funeral of Elmina Shepard Taylor, first president of the Church's young women, President Joseph F. Smith commented, "I have known a few men and women in the world who do not seek borrowed light, for the light is in them, and they walk in the light, and they have fellowship with Jesus Christ and their associates. . . . All [Elmina's] thoughts and all her energies were directed in the right channel for the right cause."[1]

As a young woman, Elmina sought to know the truth and to be baptized by immersion, which she described as the "pattern set by our Savior." Before reading the Book of Mormon, she prayed to know whether or not it was true. Realizing that her life would change dramatically were she to join an unpopular religion, yet unable to "silence [her] convictions,"[2] twenty-five-year-old Elmina was baptized on July 5, 1856. She had implicit faith in the promise, "If you will obey the doctrine, you shall know whether it is of God or man." This faith served her well throughout her life, particularly during the twenty-four years she served as the first general president of the Young Ladies' National Mutual Improvement Association (YLMIA).

A New York Childhood

Anstis Elmina Shepard was born in Middlefield, Otsego County, New York, on September 12, 1830, just a few months after The Church of Jesus Christ of Latter-day Saints was organized. Her parents, David Spaulding and Rozella Bailey Shepard, staunch members of the Methodist Episcopal Church, were regarded as honest and respectable members of their community.[3] Before Elmina's birth, they had lost a son, Alfred, who died in infancy; they subsequently had two additional daughters, Ann and Hannah.

Elmina — or Mina, as her family and friends called her — was frail in health but strong in her convictions. Some of her earliest memories were of riding to church in a sleigh in the winter and of reading the Bible with her family. She loved nature and often walked in the woods near her home, stopping occasionally to pray, giving thanks and asking for blessings for her family and herself.[4] Part of her childhood was spent on her grandparents' farm in a heavily wooded area of upstate New York, which in the summer had a profusion of flowers, maple and cherry trees, streams, and birds.

Elmina attended public school and then Hardwick Academy, where she was awarded a teaching diploma at age sixteen. For several years she taught school in rural areas, receiving payment in the form of board and room at students' homes. Not liking this practice, she found a more lucrative position through her cousin, Kate McLane, who was teaching in southern New York. Her new school in Haverstraw was two hundred miles from Middlefield. Her parents initially forbade her to go; when they finally relented, she set out in midwinter on her first train ride. She and Kate boarded together in a home in Haverstraw, on the west side of the Hudson River not far from New York City. Elmina enjoyed this beautiful setting in the foothills of the Catskill Mountains, with sailboats and steamers plying the river and elegant summer homes of wealthy New Yorkers dotting its banks.

At age twenty, Elmina joined the Methodist church, to which her parents belonged, and for the next five and a half years she worked actively in the church, although she questioned some doctrines and practices. When she posed questions to her minister, especially about baptism by immersion, his answers confused her even more.

Conversion and Marriage

During the four years she lived in Haverstraw, Elmina became friends with John Druce, a trustee of the school. An elder in The Church of Jesus Christ of Latter-day Saints, he gave her a copy of the Book of Mormon and other literature, with the admonition, "You know the Bible says 'prove all things; and hold fast that which is good.' "[5] As she studied, she came to believe, and in 1856 she joined the Church. Reflecting on her conversion, she later said, "When I was confirmed by the laying on of hands I received the testimony of [the gospel's] truth which I have never lost from that day to this."[6]

Through John Druce, Elmina also met George Hamilton Taylor, a young copper engraver who boarded at the Druce home. He too had been introduced to the gospel by John Druce and had been converted. In his autobiography, George described his early memories of Elmina and her cousin Kate:

"Miss Shepard was of a very lively vivacious disposition, witty, and ever ready at repartee. She was always the favorite whenever the two [Elmina and Kate] were out together and was always able to 'hold her own' (as the saying is) in any company in which she might be placed. Being myself a direct opposite to these characteristics in her, I soon became very much interested in her, and thought that I would be supremely happy if I could get her for a wife. But I was of such a timid, bashful disposition, and so fearful of being refused, that when in the company of both of them, I paid nearly all my attention to Miss McLane. And I carried this to such a length that Miss Shepard thought that I did not care anything for her, while her cousin thought that I was in earnest in giving her seemingly the preference. I did not act thus to deceive Miss McLane, but as a blind to cover my real feelings from Miss Shepard, until I could discover whether there was any prospect of success if I undertook openly to win her."[7]

When Kate went home for a visit, George was finally able to spend time alone with Elmina and express his true feelings for her. Persistent in his courting, he noted, "It was but a few weeks before I had gained her consent to be my wife."[8] They were betrothed February 14, 1856. Kate, upon her return, was furious, feeling that both George and Elmina had deceived her, and she soon left Haverstraw. George and Elmina never heard from her again.

When Elmina joined the Church, one school trustee did

not want to renew her teaching contract, though another trustee commented that he "did not care whether she was a Catholic, Protestant or Mormon, she had kept the best school they had ever had in that district."[9]

Elmina and George decided they would not be married until she finished her current teaching contract; she also wanted to visit her grandparents in upstate New York. However, the day before she was to leave, Elders John Taylor and George A. Smith of the Quorum of the Twelve Apostles visited the Druce home and urged the couple to marry immediately. And so George and Elmina were married August 31, 1856, by Elder Taylor, and the next morning she set out for her grandparents' home. George followed her there a month later.

The newlyweds, apparently hesitant to tell her grandparents that not only were they now Mormons but they were also married, kept their marriage a secret and were married again at the grandparents' home. George later wrote, "If we had known as much then . . . as we did afterwards, we would not have gone through the [second] ceremony. But however wrong it was from a religious stand point, our motives were good, as we wished to conciliate them, and take away some of the sting of our joining an unpopular people."[10]

After this second wedding ceremony, the couple traveled to Bloomfield, New Jersey, so George could introduce his bride to his parents. His mother later told him that she herself could not have found a more suitable wife for him. Elmina then traveled to Wisconsin to visit her parents, who had moved there from New York (George, however, did not meet his in-laws for several more years).

George and Elmina lived in Haverstraw for the next two and a half years while they prepared to join the Saints in Salt Lake City. In April 1859 they were finally ready to bid farewell to the small community where, George said, "we had spent so many pleasant years, and where so much had transpired to change the current of our lives."[11]

The trip to Salt Lake City took five months and involved a variety of modes of travel, including train, steamboat, covered wagon, and on foot. En route to Winter Quarters, near Omaha, Nebraska, they detoured to Ripon, Wisconsin, to visit Elmina's

family. The only Latter-day Saint in her family, she related to
them a prophecy given to her that they would all be reunited.[12]

At Winter Quarters, George was initiated into how to handle
oxen and a wagon, while Elmina became quickly immersed in
housekeeping—her first such experience, since her entire married life they had boarded at a home in Haverstraw. As the
couple did not have children, four other people were assigned
to their wagon: a young man who was mentally handicapped,
an asthmatic English widow, a thirty-year-old German woman
who spoke no English, and an older single woman, who, as
George described her, "said she was a descendent of the Salem
witches, and her looks and actions did not belie her descent."
"With this singular crowd we started," he said, "all on foot except
Mina, who rode in the well-loaded wagon on the 26th day of
June 1859. . . . We were strung along, (60 wagons of us) for over
a mile, and the antics of wild cattle, and green drivers, was
something to remember for a lifetime."[13]

Home in the Valley

On the afternoon of September 16, 1859, the pioneer company arrived in the Salt Lake Valley, eighty-two days after leaving
Winter Quarters. Other members of the wagon train were met
by family members or friends, but George and Elmina knew no
one. Desolate and lonely, they sat on the tongue of their wagon
until Elder John Taylor and his wife, Maggie, invited them to
supper. Another man offered them employment, George as a
mill worker and Elmina as a cook, in Big Cottonwood Canyon.
A one-room house, shared with another family, came with their
jobs. Though Elmina found the filthy building intolerable—the
cracks between the logs were so large that mice crawled in every
night and ate their shoestrings as well as their food—she cheerfully began cleaning and making improvements. She recalled
one terrifying night when she was alone in the cabin during a
sudden thunderstorm. George had been detained at the sawmill
and could not get word to her, and she lay awake all night,
worried about her missing husband and terrified of the thunder
and lightning.[14]

With winter approaching and the mill work completed for

the season, Elmina and George next moved to the Sugar House area, about five miles southeast of the temple block in Salt Lake City. But George could find very little work, and they barely scraped through the winter. On April 1, 1860, they made a special trip in the city to be rebaptized (a common practice at the time) and to attend the Endowment House, where they received their endowments and were sealed by Brigham Young. After the ceremony, President Young invited them to dinner at his home.

In hopes of finding better job opportunities, that spring the couple moved closer to the city center. When she saw the dirty two-room home George had rented for them, Elmina cried. But, as before, she started scrubbing and repairing, and George whitewashed the walls with clay. John and Maggie Taylor visited them, and Elder Taylor commented that the Taylors "could make a comfortable home out of any kind of place."[15]

Since most of George's work was paid in store pay or tithing office goods, he and Elmina began a cottage industry to generate cash. An experienced copper engraver, he cut wood blocks and stamped baby clothes for embroidery, which the couple gave to some of their friends. Word spread, and soon the couple had as much work as they could handle. They also made baby clothes in anticipation of the arrival of their first child, George Shepard Taylor, who was born July 16, 1860.

George worked at a variety of jobs to provide for his family, but most often he made sashes and doors, trading his work for food and materials with which to build his own house. Not long after their second son, Frank David, was born in September 1862, the family moved to their partially completed home. Snow fell before George got the roof on, and all through the winter, Elmina would hold a tallow candle so he could see at night to plane boards by hand and to tongue and groove them to finish the floor. It took them three years to complete the house with plaster and paint. "In the meantime," according to George, "the bugs had got into the adobe walls, and we suffered fearfully, for we could not get at them."[16] Nevertheless, Elmina, who loved the beauties of nature and missed the lush greenery of the Hudson River Valley, beautified her new home by planting a large flower garden bordered by climbing roses.

A skilled and hard worker, George was in demand and

received offers from several businessmen to form a company. Instead, he decided to start his own lumber company. He had machinery, the first in the territory, shipped in from the East. The company prospered the first year and made a significant profit, which George put toward his debt for the machinery. During the winter he stockpiled a large supply of doors and sashes, but disaster struck: the building caught fire and everything, including the machinery, burned. Determined to succeed, George started over, working by hand until the machinery could be salvaged and rebuilt.

During these years, five more children were born to Elmina and George: Lydia Rosella, October 2, 1864; Erminnie Mae, February 9, 1867; Clarence Warren, January 22, 1869; Elmina Mae, August 11, 1871; and Eugene L., January 10, 1874. Lydia Rosella and Erminnie died two days apart, in September 1867, and Eugene died three days after birth, leaving the couple with three sons and a daughter to raise.

The Taylors also welcomed Elmina's parents and her sister Ann, who came to live with them in 1872. This fulfilled the prophecy made to Elmina years before, although none of her family ever joined the Church. The year after they arrived in the valley, her father, mother, and sister became ill with smallpox, which George described as "of the most violent type," and which "seemed to be the greatest trial that we had been subjected to."[17] Elmina's mother died from the dreaded disease in June 1873; her father and sister eventually recovered.

A Principle Embraced

Twenty years after their marriage, George and Elmina agreed to enter into the practice of plural marriage. Speaking for both Elmina and himself, George wrote in his autobiography, "We had rather [polygamy] were not a principle of our religion, yet we knew the principles we had embraced were true, and as that came from the same source we could not reject it. So we came to the conclusion that as it did not affect us at the present time, and if it ever did, it would be in the distant future, we would not exact, or give any promises in relation to the matter. But [we] would go forward, live our religion, keep the commandments of God, and strive to do right in all things, as far as we knew how, trusting that if the time ever came when we should embrace that principle and practice it, that we should know it and be prepared for it."[18]

With Elmina's consent, George began courting Lois Louise (Louie) Foote, "stating fairly and squarely, my situation and circumstances and object at the start."[19] Elmina welcomed her as a sister wife, noting in her diary: "July 4th, 1877, we entered into the celestial order of marriage, and have since all lived under the same roof, and eaten at the same table, ever in the enjoyment of peace and harmony."[20]

In December 1878 George was called by the First Presidency on a mission to England. In his absence Elmina had to care for her own four children in addition to Louie and her new baby, and also to keep George's lumber business going. She recorded her feelings of loneliness in her diary. On June 24, 1879, she wrote: "Again more than usual shall I miss my dear Husband. I am very lonely tonight." On August 21, 1879: "Someone sang Maggie dear[.] Immediately was I carried back to Haverstraw and the tears sprang to my eyes and my heart gave a great throb. I was sitting by your side, riding up the Long Clove and you were singing it to me with a *slight* change in words and a heart full of love. While my mind was thus busy Mae looked up in my face and whispered, Papa sings that. So you see every slight event brings to mind our absent loved one."[21] Martha Horne Tingey said of George and Elmina's close and loving relationship, "Their gentle consideration for each other's feelings, the sincere affection manifested in every little word and act, which is so much more expressive than any loud or special demonstration, was an inspiration."[22]

In September 1880, after serving in the mission field for nearly three years, George sailed to New York City, where Elmina surprised him by meeting him at the dock. After visiting his family in New Jersey, they returned to Salt Lake City by train.

In 1885, George married his third wife, Ellen Susannah (Nellie) Colebrooke, a widow from England. The following year he, along with many other prominent Latter-day Saint men, was arrested for cohabitation, tried, and sentenced to prison. The Fourteenth Ward held a farewell reception for him before he began serving his six-month sentence. Following his release, he was called to serve as bishop of the ward.

A Beloved Leader

Though she had her hands full with a growing family, particularly while George was in England, Elmina always found time to serve in the Church. When the Fourteenth Ward Relief Society was organized in December 1867, she was selected as secretary, a position she held for twenty-six years. In September 1874, she was called to lead the Young Ladies' Retrenchment Association in her ward. And in 1879, she became first counselor in the Salt Lake Stake Relief Society, a position she held for sixteen years. For several years she served in all three of these positions simultaneously.

Elmina's abilities and willingness to serve were observed by Eliza R. Snow, the general president of the Relief Society. Of one encounter Elmina recorded in her diary in 1879: "Sr. Snow clasped me in her arms and said she always felt like blessing me all over, because I am such a faithful worker in the Kingdom. I fear I do not merit it but will strive to in the future."[23] Sister Snow herself held several positions simultaneously, having led the Relief Society since its reorganization in the Salt Lake Valley in 1866, the Retrenchment Society (later renamed the Young Ladies' National Mutual Improvement Association) since its organization in 1869, and the Primary since its organization in 1878.

On June 19, 1880, to commemorate Brigham Young's birthday, President John Taylor called a special sisters' conference in the Assembly Hall on Temple Square. The purpose of the meeting was to organize general presidencies and boards for each of these auxiliaries.

At the morning session of the conference, Louie B. Felt was named the president of the Primary Association. Between the morning and afternoon meetings of the conference, Elmina had lunch at the home of Bathsheba W. Smith, who was the treasurer of the Salt Lake Stake Relief Society, with Mary Isabella Horne, the stake Relief Society president, and Sister Snow. Elmina recounted their discussion:

"We were talking of the organization of the Young Ladies' Central Board, and Sister Snow said, 'Have you chosen your counselors?'

"I said, 'Counselors for what?'

"Sister Snow answered, 'We are going to put you in as president of all the [Young Ladies'] associations.'

" 'I shall not act,' I replied.

"We ate dinner.

"Sister Snow said, 'Have you chosen them?'

"I said I would not and could not.

"Sister Snow said, 'Well, if you won't, we'll choose them for you.'

"I said, 'Well, if I have to act, I'll choose them myself.' "[24]

At the afternoon meeting of the conference, Elmina was sustained as the first general president of the YLMIA, and Eliza R. Snow was retained as the Relief Society president. As her counselors, Elmina chose Margaret (Maggie) Young Taylor, wife of John Taylor, the first person who befriended her when she arrived in the valley, and twenty-two-year-old Martha Horne, a daughter of Mary Isabella Horne. Louie Wells was called as secretary, and Fannie Young Thatcher as treasurer.

As the new YLMIA president, Elmina was instructed to "find new and surprising ways . . . to teach girls how to develop every gift and grace of true womanhood."[25] Throughout her term of office, she found it difficult to speak publicly but gathered her courage when faced with the task. She once told her associates, "When young lady officers are asked to preside or to sit upon the stand, they should accept such invitation, no matter if it be a trial."[26] In her first address as president of the YLMIA, she said: "Our young people should also be ladies and gentlemen, and we should educate them in all the sciences of the day that they may not be behind in any good thing. Mothers, look after your daughters, keep them near you, keep their confidence—that they may be true and faithful, and that our associations may not languish and pine in the future as they have in the past."[27]

For Elmina, to serve as the first president of the association was a pioneering venture, for the territory was uncharted and untraveled. There were no precedents to follow and no previous experience to rely upon. As Susa Young Gates noted in the

History of Y.L.M.I.A., "There was no General Board, no aids, no guides, no magazine nor other publications for their work; no quarterly or yearly conferences nor conventions, either stake or general; no headquarters, not even any regular meetings of the general officers."[28]

One of Elmina's first challenges was bringing unity and uniformity to the various associations scattered throughout the Church, for each local association had been autonomous, planning its own programs and procedures. The general presidency and board at first decided to meet quarterly, but they soon found it necessary to meet more frequently.

During the first ten years of Elmina's administration, her board often met with the officers of the Salt Lake Stake YLMIA, which had been functioning for a number of years. The more experienced stake leaders shared their insights with the new central board. (The term *central board* was changed in 1921 to *general board,* and *aids* became known as *general board members.)*

At first the YLMIA program was offered only during the winter months, but as stakes felt the need for a summer program, they were encouraged to submit plans for approval. Classwork involved lessons in theology, literature, domestic science, parliamentary procedure, and good manners.

As YLMIA president, Elmina made hundreds of visits during the first ten years of her presidency, traveling thousands of miles by team and wagon. Her companions often included counselors or board members as well as representatives of the other auxiliary organizations: Eliza R. Snow, general president of the Relief Society; Zina D. H. Young, counselor in the Relief Society presidency; Sarah M. Kimball, general secretary of the Relief Society; Emmeline B. Wells, editor of the *Woman's Exponent;* Mary Isabella Horne, president of the Salt Lake Stake Relief Society; and Louie B. Felt, Primary general president. The visitors organized new associations, held conferences, gave instructions, and gathered ideas from the field. Elmina was not strong physically and, much to her dismay, at times she could not travel. Other times, she ignored her family's pleas not to travel because of her ill health. Her daughter, Mae Taylor Nystrom, noted, however, that

Elmina "always returned home stronger in body and uplifted in spirit."[29]

To finance the general organization and the travel of its leaders, each YLMIA member was asked to contribute a dime each year to a special fund. At first stakes retained one-fourth of the money collected, but later the whole amount was sent to Salt Lake City to meet increasing costs of the central organization. The stakes then raised their own funds, primarily through fairs and bazaars. Some stakes assessed wards a yearly sum.

Not until January 1888, eight years after they were called to their respective positions, were the members of the YLMIA general presidency set apart. President Wilford Woodruff set apart Elmina. His counselors, George Q. Cannon and Joseph F. Smith, set apart her counselors, Maria Young Dougall, who had replaced Margaret Taylor as first counselor in 1887, and Martha Horne Tingey. (Martha, who had been single when she was originally called as second counselor, had married Joseph S. Tingey in 1884.) When Louie Wells died in 1887, Mary E. Cook became the general secretary, and Ann M. Cannon, assistant secretary. After Mary moved from Salt Lake City in 1891, Ann replaced her as secretary. Nellie Colebrooke Taylor, Elmina's husband's third wife, served on the central board.

In 1889 Susa Young Gates, a member of the central board who was serving a mission in the Sandwich Islands (Hawaii) with her husband, wrote to the First Presidency about publishing a magazine for young women. After conferring with Elmina, who was enthusiastic about the project, the Brethren gave their permission and appointed Susa as editor. The first issue of the monthly *Young Woman's Journal* appeared in October 1889. A subscription cost one dollar a year. Elmina saw the magazine as a way to communicate more effectively with young women and their leaders.

At first local associations developed their own programs and lessons, but in 1890 the central officers and board outlined a schedule for weekly meetings:

1. Singing (Association choir, prayer, and roll call)
2. Miscellaneous business
3. Bible lecture

4. Historical narrative or biographical sketch
5. Musical exercise
6. Book of Mormon, alternating with Church history
7. Answering questions
8. Declamation [recitation], alternating with select reading
9. Report of current events or an essay
10. Scientific lecture
11. Distribution of queries and reading programme
12. Closing exercise, singing, benediction[30]

The first guide or manual, with lessons and instructions "to set the young ladies to thinking on definite topics," was published in pamphlet form in 1893.[31] Three courses of study were included in each year's lessons, one always on theology and the other two on such subjects as history, literature, physical culture, domestic science, physiology, and ethics.[32] Beginning in 1897, the lessons were published in the *Young Woman's Journal*.

Another literary effort, traveling libraries, began during Elmina's administration. The concept of traveling libraries was for stakes to collect good books and circulate them among the wards to encourage young women to read.

Unifying the YLMIA

The second decade of Elmina Taylor's administration was marked by the development of uniformity in the programs and the associations. After the *Young Woman's Journal* was launched, the general presidency had a means of communicating monthly with the wards and stakes. At the beginning of the 1890s, the YLMIA had 300 branches with 8,000 members. By the turn of the century, membership had grown to 485 associations with 20,575 members in the United States, Canada, Mexico, England, New Zealand, and Hawaii.

Elmina presided over the first general YLMIA conference on April 4, 1890, in Salt Lake City, commemorating the tenth anniversary of the organization.[33] The presidency explained the purpose of YLMIA in the May 1891 *Young Woman's Journal*: "The aim of the leaders of this movement has been to cultivate every gift and grace of true womanhood, recognizing the fact that it is not the outward appearance but the forces which gather within the soul that go to develop the individual. To this end every effort is made to induce independent thought, study, individuality and progress. Great stress is laid upon the physical well-being of woman."[34]

The YLMIA joined with the Relief Society in affiliating with the National Council of Women in 1891. Elmina, who was elected an ex-officio vice president, attended several conventions in the East and presided over a meeting on behalf of the YLMIA at the Chicago World's Fair in 1893.

In 1893, Tuesday night was designated as "Mutual" night throughout the Church. One night a month the YLMIA and YMMIA met jointly for speech development. Later, opening exercises, during which the young men and women met together before they separated to classes, were added to the program. In 1896, the YLMIA and YMMIA held their first combined conference in the Salt Lake Tabernacle. This was the beginning of June Conference, an annual event that would continue until 1975. President Joseph F. Smith, a member of the First Presidency, addressed the first conference and said that the women should be as knowledgeable as the men about the gospel.

With the Church becoming an international organization, the word *National* was dropped from the title of the young ladies' organization in 1904, making its official name the Young Ladies' Mutual Improvement Association.

Elmina was much loved by her co-workers and the girls she served. In July 1894, the Salt Lake Stake YLMIA hosted a surprise party for her, attended by President Lorenzo Snow, several apostles, the YLMIA counselors and general board members, members of the other auxiliary presidenies, and the young women of the Salt Lake Stake. Elmina was indeed surprised, for she thought she was attending a Young Ladies' social. The YLMIA presented her with an album containing tributes from ward presidents.

To commemorate Elmina's birthday, at the 1894 October general conference the YLMIA designated September 12 as Annual Day. Besides honoring Elmina, Annual Day's purpose was to unite the young women in participation in outdoor games and sports. In 1904 Annual Day was held jointly for young men and young women. Seven years later, in 1911, the name was changed to Field Day, and the activity was moved to June to coincide with June Conference.

Unable to travel during her later years because of ill health, Elmina felt she was not doing all she should as YLMIA president and offered to let someone else "more competent," as she termed it, take her place. Though she was so weak that she had to lie on a couch during board meetings, she continued to direct the meetings, listening attentively to the various reports from board members who had visited conferences and conventions. And, as the *Young Woman's Journal* reported, she "never failed to have a decided opinion on [any subject], and one which every member of her board knew to be inspired."[35] Elmina received several blessings from the General Authorities. In one blessing given by Elder George Teasdale in May 1899, she was promised "the spirit of life, health, comfort, and peace": "The Lord shall bless thee, heal thee, comfort thee, make thee strong and prolong thy days upon the earth; for thou shalt live upon the earth until thou art satisfied with life, and then thou shalt depart like an innocent child into peaceful sleep."[36] She attended to YLMIA business up to the day before her death.

Elmina Shepard Taylor died peacefully on December 6, 1904, at the age of seventy-four, having served as general president of the YLMIA for twenty-four and a half years. At her funeral in the Assembly Hall on December 11, a blanket of flowers, representing each of the Young Ladies' groups throughout the Church, covered her casket, along with an American Beauty rose laid by each general board member.

Elmina related well to the young women she served, and in her they found a gracious, faithful Latter-day Saint. An example of the admonition she gave the YLMIA leaders — "to be kind rather than harsh, complimentary rather than critical"[37] — she always endeavored to follow her convictions: to live by the light she gained as a young woman seeking the truth.

2

Martha Horne Tingey
1905–1929

When Martha Jane Horne received her patriarchal blessing as a young woman, she was promised that she would perform a great work among youth. The blessing also revealed that the adversary would seek to prevent her from fulfilling this mission and would even attempt to take her life. However, she was assured that if she put her trust in the Lord and always kept his commandments, she would have the power to overcome the adversary and to successfully perform her work with the youth.[1]

The fulfillment of this blessing is evidenced by the fact that Martha, whose physical health was generally weak, served for forty-eight years in the presidency of the YLMIA—longer than any other YLMIA leader. Family, friends, and co-workers repeatedly acknowledged that her faith and strong spirit gave her the strength to carry out her responsibilities. A tribute by YLMIA board member Emma Goddard, written for Martha's seventieth birthday, typifies how many felt about her. Emma wrote, "I have loved you [Martha] for the fortitude and patience with which you have borne your sorrows."[2]

Heritage and Childhood

Martha was born October 15, 1857, in Salt Lake City, Utah, to Joseph and Mary Isabella Hales Horne. Both Joseph and Mary Isabella were born in England and immigrated as children, with their families, to Toronto, Ontario, Canada, in the early nineteenth century. They were married in Toronto on May 9, 1836.

A month after their marriage, they heard the gospel preached by missionary brothers Orson and Parley P. Pratt. They immediately responded to the truthfulness of the gospel message and were baptized by Orson Hyde on July 6. The following year, the couple joined the Saints in Missouri and eventually moved with them to Nauvoo, Illinois; Winter Quarters, Nebraska; and the Salt Lake Valley.

By the time Martha—or Mattie, as she would be known throughout her life—was born, the Hornes were well established in Salt Lake City. She was the fourteenth child born into this family of fifteen, which included three sets of twins. The Hornes enjoyed entertaining guests in their home, and Mattie, spiritually mature for her age, enjoyed sitting quietly in a corner and listening to the testimonies of those who visited. As a result, she became acquainted with many Church leaders.

A fine seamstress, Mary Isabella taught her daughter to sew and also embroider, an interest Mattie pursued throughout her life. These hours of sewing together and the love both shared for books and music resulted in an especially close relationship, which they maintained as adults.

Mattie's remarkable abilities in speaking and music became evident early in her life. Her talent as a public speaker was noticeable almost as soon as she learned to read. Educated at home by her older sisters and in the ward school, she quickly mastered the alphabet and primer and became an avid reader at a time when books were not readily available—so avid, in fact, that her mother sometimes had to take her books away from her and send her outside to play. Mattie wrote: "I read all the histories and everything else in the Sunday School library as well as all other books that came in my way. I used to read aloud to mother, and to visitors many times, which has been a great benefit to me, and is a practice I would recommend to mothers to encourage in their children."[3]

As a schoolgirl, Mattie won many awards for her achievements in reading, spelling, and arithmetic. At age eight, she won an award in a speech competition against students from three other schools. Mattie, who had a clear, strong voice and an amazing capacity to memorize long passages, was often asked to stand and recite poems at school. In Sunday School she would recite as many as forty verses from the Bible or Doctrine and Covenants. On one occasion she read a poem at a party given in honor of Eliza R. Snow, then president of the Relief Society, shortly after Eliza's return from the Holy Land. Friends praised Mattie on "the tender sweetness of her tones and the music of her intonation."[4] That she was so eloquent was especially remarkable because her timid nature was a personal challenge for her. Performing in front of others required a great deal of courage.

Mattie's musical talents became apparent early in her life. She frequently sang in small gatherings, and she joined the ward choir at age fourteen. On January 19, 1877, at age twenty, she was accepted in the Tabernacle Choir. In addition to singing with the choir for fourteen years, she continued to sing in her own and other wards.

Spiritually mature for her age, Mattie had many opportunities to serve in the Church while she was still in her teens. A member of the Salt Lake Fourteenth Ward, she served as a counselor in the Primary. At sixteen, soon after she began attending the Retrenchment Association, she was called to serve as a counselor in the presidency. Two years later she began teaching a Sunday School class of young ladies, with whom she became very close during the nine years she served as their teacher.

After her early schooling at home and in the ward school, Mattie took classes for two years at the University of Deseret (now the University of Utah). An unexpected educational opportunity came in the summer of 1873, when she was sixteen. President Brigham Young and Elder George Q. Cannon invited six young ladies to learn the trade of typesetting. "This was a departure, even for the progressive Mormons," Susa Young Gates, editor of the *Young Woman's Journal,* wrote of the venture, "and much was said to discourage the innovation."[5] But Mattie had both the attitude and the aptitude for the job and thus was not surprised to find her name at the top of the list of young women recommended by Brigham Young for the training.

Mattie's typesetting abilities led to a position at the *Deseret News,* where "she donned a printer's apron over her ankle-length skirt and starched white blouse and learned to pick lead letters from the compartments in the waist-high case and line them up in a compositor's stick. Many scoffed at the idea of young women working in the printing shop of the *Deseret News,* but Mattie learned to ignore any remarks made to her and take comfort in the fact that her foreman had told her she was one of the best compositors he had."[6]

Courtship, Marriage, and Family Life

Among those who did not scoff at the young female type-setters was Joseph S. Tingey. Though Joseph worked in another area of the newspaper office, he looked for opportunities to be with Mattie. By 1880 they had become good friends and fond of one another. However, that year their lives took different directions: Joseph left for the British Mission, and Mattie was called on June 19 to serve as a counselor to the first YLMIA general president, Elmina S. Taylor. Mattie continued to work as a typesetter, teach her Sunday School class of young ladies, and sing in the Tabernacle Choir during the first years she served in this new position.

Joseph returned from his mission in 1882 and was pleased to find Mattie still unmarried. Their mutual attraction deepened, and on September 30, 1884, they were married in the Salt Lake Temple. After their marriage, Joseph continued to work at the *Deseret News* as a printer, but Mattie, who had been employed for ten years, gave up her job in order to stay home and rear a family.

After Mattie gave birth to her first child, Joseph, Jr., on October 28, 1885, she suffered a serious setback in her health. She apparently had a hip problem that was aggravated by child-birth, and she had also dislocated her right kneecap. Her doctor informed her that if she survived these complications, she might never be able to walk again.[7] While her recovery was slow, it was filled with tender care and frequent priesthood blessings by her husband. Her patriarchal blessing, which had promised her the power to overcome the adversary and successfully per-form her work with the youth if she put her trust in the Lord, gave her the faith that she would someday fully recover. Though she had a noticeable limp the rest of her life, she did, in fact, eventually walk again and without a cane. She was able to resume her responsibilities in homemaking, raising a family, and serving in the Church, though she suffered from bouts of ill health the rest of her life.

The Tingeys became the parents of five more children: William, born May 17, 1889; twins Clarence and Clara, born December 18, 1891; twins Weiler and Stafford, born on April 10, 1897 (they died eighteen days later); and Rulon, born November 24, 1899.[8]

Mattie's priorities clearly placed her family first. "Can you think of any better, broader field of action than that of wife and mother?" she wrote, "or any labor that will reap such a glorious harvest?"[9] Susa Young Gates noted that Mattie was "devoted to her home and family and [was] known among her associates as a good wife and mother. Martha [had] the unusual quality of system and order, so that all her tasks fell into line as well-drilled soldiers."[10]

While her children were young, Mattie relied heavily upon her husband, Joseph, for comfort and support. "[Their] union has been very congenial and one of mutual helpfulness," wrote Susa Young Gates. "Brother Tingey's liberal character is an example of what a man can do, as a husband, father and Elder in Israel, without in any way hindering the development of a gifted wife."[11]

Joseph and Mattie were well-matched and happy in their marriage. Life for members of the Tingey family was likewise happy, testifying to the fact that Joseph and Mattie managed to maintain a stable family relationship in spite of Mattie's travel and other responsibilities with the YLMIA and Joseph's own responsibilities as a bishop. All of the children remembered their home as a place of peace.[12]

Gospel teachings were important in the Tingey home. One Sunday, when the boys wanted to know why they couldn't play baseball, Mattie reminded them that her sons "never put themselves among a pleasure-loving group on Sunday."[13]

Mattie had her own ideas about how her sons should leave on their missions: she believed they should leave from and return to their home. Clarence remembered that she would hug each of her sons and then wave from the doorway, rather than going to the train station for good-byes. When each of the missionaries returned, she waited for them at home with bread baking in the oven.[14]

Twenty-four Years as a Counselor

When twenty-two-year-old Mattie was called in 1880 to serve as Elmina Taylor's second counselor in the YLMIA presidency, she could not have guessed she would remain in that position for twenty-four years. Elmina, a close friend of Mattie's mother, had known Mattie for many years and was well aware of her strong spiritual nature, her intellect, and her talents in speech and music. The strength of Mattie's gifts outweighed any disadvantages incident to her youth and lack of experience.

In the presidency, Mattie bridged a peculiar gap: the women she served with were close to the age of her mother, while the young women in the program were close to her own age. This occasionally presented a problem for her. For example, although dancing had always been an appropriate part of pioneer recreation, the waltz and round dance were discouraged in 1883. Still single, she loved to dance and identified with the feelings and interests of the youth. However, her service in the YLMIA presidency put her in contact with the thinking of adult women. Her youthful viewpoint no doubt influenced the leaders, while at the same time the leaders' mature viewpoint tempered her enthusiasm. Obedient, she refrained from encouraging the waltz and the round dance. But time was on her side, for these dances eventually gained general acceptance and won their way into the YLMIA program during her administration.

As Mattie matured with marriage and motherhood, her strengths blossomed. "Mrs. Tingey is always a convincing speaker, and at times pours forth her soul in the true language of eloquence," Susa Young Gates wrote of her. "She has a dignified manner, and is quiet in speech, though aggressive in her opinions. She has the prudence to restrain speech, when silence is golden. If asked to name the most marked trait in Mrs. Tingey's character, the answer would be, sincerity, genuineness."[15]

Though for several years her health problems prevented

her from traveling, Mattie became a well-known spokeswoman for the YLMIA. When she was finally well enough to travel outside the Salt Lake Valley, she bore a strong testimony of "the power of healing manifested in her behalf through the ordinances of the Holy Priesthood."[16]

In October 1888 Mattie spoke at a conference of the Young Men's and Young Ladies' associations in the Salt Lake Tabernacle. Emmeline B. Wells, editor of the *Woman's Exponent*, wrote of this occasion: "Mrs. Tingey made an eloquent speech that attracted the attention of the large congregation assembled there; in fact, she seemed fairly to outdo herself, and her earnest words thrilled the hearts of the audience and produced a telling if not a lasting effect."[17]

In a speech at the Congress of Women held during the 1893 World's Fair at Chicago, Mattie shared her vision of womanhood: "Let woman prepare herself to stand side by side, shoulder to shoulder with her husband in all the affairs of life, to be a wise counselor and helpmeet unto him, as her Creator designed she should be. . . . Woman herself is beginning to feel that she is an intelligence, with talents that it is her duty to develop and use for the advancement and elevation of the human family. This feeling is gradually but steadily growing; it is being felt throughout the world, and it will continue to grow until it becomes a power in the earth."[18]

As a counselor, Mattie was a strong spokesman for the YLMIA. For example, when Annual Day was instituted in 1894 as a day for the young women to join with their parents in "relaxing amusement," she encouraged the young women to bring a dime to donate to the general YLMIA fund. "It is not only the dime but the heart of the girls we want," said Mattie. "They should be educated to the principle that it is a privilege to pay."[19]

General President of the YLMIA

In 1904, shortly after Elmina S. Taylor died, Mattie was called to serve as president of the YLMIA. When President Joseph F. Smith set her apart to preside over the YLMIA, he pronounced a blessing upon her, promising her she would have health and strength to perform her labors. A comment written by Susa Young Gates testified to the fulfillment of that blessing: "For years her [Mattie's] health had been of the most precarious nature, but from the day when she came by faith and will-power to take her place after the funeral of her leader Sister Taylor, Sister Tingey has rarely been absent at any of the many and taxing councils of her Board."[20]

Mattie's choice of counselors helped make the fulfillment of this blessing possible. Ruth May Fox, healthy and vigorous, became first counselor. Her energy allowed her to travel to areas outside of Salt Lake City. She not only served with Mattie for the entire twenty-four years of her presidency, but also succeeded her as the president of the YLMIA in 1929. Mae Taylor Nystrom, Harvard-educated daughter of Elmina Taylor, served as second counselor for eighteen years and gave invaluable loyalty and support to Mattie. Following Mae's release in 1923, Lucy Grant Cannon became second counselor. Young and capable, Lucy willingly helped Mattie shoulder the burdens of the presidency for the remaining six years of her administration. Her ability to drive a car became a valuable asset during this time when few families owned a car and few women knew how to drive.

On August 25, 1905, only four months after Mattie was called to serve as YLMIA president, her mother, Mary Isabella Horne, died at the age of eighty-seven. Mattie felt a void in her life without her mother and the close forty-eight-year relationship she had had with her, first as an obedient daughter, next as an eager student, later as a close friend, and finally as a co-worker in the Church, with Mary Isabella a member of the Relief Society general board and Mattie in the presidency of the YLMIA. Often others had noticed the similarities between the two women and described them in comments such as these by Susa Young Gates: "Mrs. Tingey inherit[ed] her mother's firm, wise temperament," and "She [Mattie] is rather small in stature, with the same gentle but firm voice and manner which were so much a part of her mother."[21]

One of Mattie's first goals as YLMIA president was "to visit every stake in the Church and to look upon the inspiring faces of the young women wherever they are gathered under the

Mutual banner."[22] During the first five years of her administration, she visited YLMIA members and leaders in Oregon, Wyoming, and Idaho, Canada, and Mexico. Mattie's love for the young ladies of the Church motivated her to do whatever needed to be done. "My heart is with the Mutual Improvement work," she said in an address. "I love the youth of Zion. I am anxious . . . that they may become a mighty army for righteousness in the kingdom of God."[23]

At the start of her administration, Mattie held board meetings every three months in a small room in the Constitution Building at 30 South Main Street in downtown Salt Lake City. But it wasn't long before Bathsheba W. Smith of the Relief Society and May Anderson of the Primary met with Mattie to discuss a proposed Women's Building to be built at 40 North Main, opposite the east gate of the Salt Lake Temple. The auxiliary presidents became united in their resolve to cooperate in this venture. In 1908, the plans for the building were changed to include the offices of the Presiding Bishop, and subsequently the name was changed to the Bishop's Building. When Bathsheba Smith heard the news, she reportedly fainted. However, by the time the building was completed in 1909, the Relief Society, YLMIA, and Primary leaders were happy to move into their new offices.

By then, the YLMIA had grown considerably, and it became necessary to hold weekly board meetings. Since Mattie and her husband did not own a car, for many years she rode a streetcar nearly three miles to and from her home at Eighteenth South and Main Street to the downtown office. Typical of her determination, she walked to the streetcar stop, despite her limp, and used the commuting time to read, make notes, and write speeches.

Changes in the Programs

Dramatic changes took place in the class structure for young women during Mattie's administration. Originally there were only two class divisions — the Senior and the Junior classes. After studying the Camp Fire Girls' program, YLMIA leaders developed the Beehive program in 1913. Among the things the young women had to do to advance in the Beehive program were such things as "sleep out-of-doors or with wide open windows; refrain from candy, chewing gum, sundaes, and sodas for at least two months; and, know the proper use of hot and cold baths."[24] Advancement from the Beehive class included a variety of requirements: "Pick 800 pounds of cherries or their equivalent in any six days; without help or advice, care for and harness a team at least five times; drive 50 miles in one season; and care successfully for a hive of bees for one season and know their habits."[25]

Over time, the Senior class was divided into Seniors and Advanced Seniors. Then a Junior class was added, with the rose as its symbol. In 1924 Ruth May Fox suggested that the Senior Girls be called Gleaners in honor of Ruth in the Bible. Music, elocution, literature, history, science, and systematic reading became the focus of study. Lessons on the Book of Mormon were published in the *Young Woman's Journal* for summer study. By 1910, twenty-five Mutual events were scheduled per year—fifteen class periods when lessons were presented, and ten class periods for debates, orations, and lectures.

To encourage young women to focus on a particular aspect of the gospel, a yearly slogan was approved, beginning in 1914. Among these were "We stand for a weekly home evening," 1915; "We stand for service to God and country," 1918; "We stand for a pure life through clean thought and action," 1922; "We stand for an individual test of the divinity of Jesus Christ," 1925; and "We stand for a testimony of the divine mission of Joseph Smith," 1926.

Music, drama, dance, and speech programs grew during Mattie's administration. In 1920, the first MIA-sponsored road-shows were written and performed by the Salt Lake and Ensign stakes. Young men and young women sang and danced in these lively mini-plays and then traveled with sets and costumes to another ward building within the stake to perform again for a new audience. Within a short time, roadshows were a popular activity Churchwide. The young women also learned such skills as shadow embroidery (stitching sheer fabric over embroidery) and canning. Camping took on a high profile, and by 1922 four stakes had rented land in Big Cottonwood Canyon east of Salt Lake City and built a summer home for young women at Brighton. Over the next five years, more than 4,500 young women enjoyed the facility.

In 1923, the First Presidency gave responsibility for overseeing the entire recreational program of the Church to the two Mutual Improvement Associations. June Conference in Salt Lake City was one of the yearly highlights for both workers and young women in YLMIA. Other activities focused on service projects, such as rolling bandages and collecting money for the Red Cross during World War I. In 1920 the YLMIA received permission from President Heber J. Grant to turn the Beehive House into a home for young women from out of town.

YLMIA leaders chose gold and green as the Mutual colors in 1922. "Youth is life's springtime," they said, "and springtime is always gloriously green and growing . . . and gold—[is] the color of . . . the sun." From then on, Gold and Green Balls became part of the MIA dance program.

One of the highlights of Mattie's presidency took place in 1925 when the YLMIA and the YMMIA celebrated YMMIA's Golden Jubilee. The motto for the celebration was "The glory of God is intelligence," which remained as the motto for the two organizations for many years thereafter.

During Mattie's nearly fifty years of service in the YLMIA, she saw it grow from a membership of fewer than four thousand young women to more than fifty thousand. An example of gentle leadership and of patience in disciplining her spirit, she constantly encouraged the young women to do the same. "Daughters of Zion, hold yourselves high," she told them. "Maintain your dignity and self-respect."[27]

Mattie was released on March 28, 1929, at age seventy-two. Usually silent on a subject unless she felt strongly about it, she voiced a request to the co-workers helping her clean out her desk. "Don't change the name from Young Ladies to Young Women until after I die," she said.[28]

Joy in Family

During most of Mattie's administration and afterwards, family maintained its high priority. As Joseph and Mattie's children married and had their families, grandchildren became frequent visitors at the Tingey home. "Not only did I have a 'rocking' grandmother, but I had a 'rocking and singing' grandmother," remembers Eugenia Tingey Hurlin, daughter of Mattie's son William. "I can remember her singing 'The Story of Cock Robin' to me as I sat curled up on her lap."[29]

Family gatherings at the Tingey home were festive, with lots of children, laughter, and good food. "The adults would be in the parlor playing parlor games," remembers grandson Burton S. Tingey, "and we would be in the living room playing games. Some of our games were loud and wild like Crack-the-Whip, but Grandmother let us laugh and have a good time."[30]

The Tingey home had a curving banister from the second floor to the first. "No splinters! That banister was smooth," remembers another grandson, Joseph Tingey. "Most of us grandchildren loved the thrill of sliding down that banister. And I don't ever remember Grandmother scolding us."[31]

Joseph and Mattie dearly loved their grandchildren, and the closeness of their family circle included all of them. Mattie was especially grateful for the support of her children and grandchildren when Joseph, her companion of forty-four years, died of pneumonia on July 25, 1925. After his death, Mattie's daughter, Clara, provided comfort and support to her mother. Her other children, grandchildren, and friends also helped care for her and brought happiness into her life. "All the grandchildren remember Grandmother's warm and loving welcome when we came to visit her," said grandson Burton, "even in her later years when she didn't feel well. And I'll never forget Grandmother's kitchen with its large well-stocked pantry. Grandmother and Aunt Clara kept it filled with foods that seemed to amaze me as a child."[32]

Six months before Mattie's death, her children and grandchildren gathered at her home for her eightieth birthday celebration. "I will never forget the impressive, chauffeured automobile that stopped in front of Grandmother's house that afternoon," remembers granddaughter Eugenia. "Out of the car stepped President Heber J. Grant and both of his counselors. Of course we were *shoost* into the kitchen, but I can remember peeking around the corner at Grandmother, who was laughing and visiting with the First Presidency in the parlor."[33]

Mattie died on March 11, 1938, at the age of eighty. General board member Jennie K. Mangum summed up Mattie's life when she paid her this tribute: "It is one thing to share one's money and it is better still to share one's love, but to share one's courage with those who lack faith, and who sometimes falter, or who have slipped and lose heart in the struggle — could anything be more splendid and helpful than this?"[34]

3

Ruth May Fox
1929–1937

Seventy-seven-year-old Ruth May Fox climbed Independence Rock and looked for her name. She had climbed the large granite outcropping along the pioneer trail in Wyoming some sixty-four years earlier when, as a young girl, she had walked most of the way to the Salt Lake Valley. She found her name still legible—*Ruth May, 1867.* Ruth, whose life spanned more than a century and who was both a pioneer and a modern woman, was a remarkable example to the young women of the Church of faith, commitment, and enduring to the end.

A Trying Childhood

Ruth May was born November 16, 1853, in Wiltshire, England, the first child of James and Mary Ann Harding May. Five months after her birth, her parents joined The Church of Jesus Christ of Latter-day Saints. When Ruth was just sixteen months old, her mother died in childbirth along with her baby. Mary Ann's last words to James were, "Take care of Ruth."

Although James could not care for Ruth by himself, he was anxious for her to grow up in a Latter-day Saint home. Occasionally he had her stay with relatives, but most often he arranged for Church members to take care of her. None of these arrangements lasted very long, and Ruth stayed in numerous homes and her schooling was interrupted often before she was eight years old. Her longest and last stay was with her Grandmother and Grandfather May. Then her father, who had visited her frequently, took her to Yorkshire, where he was working as a weaver. Her grandmother's parting words to James were, "She's a bad maid, she's a bad maid." Ruth, always inquisitive, had apparently tried her grandmother's patience by taking a bite out of a china saucer, catching her hair on fire with a candle, stepping in front of an oncoming train, and asking for beefsteak and beer for dinner.[1]

But James, who always saw the good in Ruth, was very proud of his pretty eight-year-old daughter, who could recite poetry and verses from the Bible. He especially enjoyed hearing her recite for friends the sixth chapter of Ephesians, which begins, "Children, obey your parents in the Lord: for this is right." (Ephesians 6:1.)

In Yorkshire, James and Ruth boarded at the home of a Latter-day Saint woman, Mary Saxton. A handsome widower, James could easily have remarried earlier, but his primary concern was in finding a new wife who would be kind to Ruth. He found such a person in Mary Saxton, who had left an abusive husband. They became engaged, and James emigrated to America in March 1865 to earn enough money to send for her, her daughter, Clara, and Ruth. Six months later he sent them funds for their ship passage. Ruth was excited about the prospects of a new home in a new land. She recalled, "It is a real sensation to board a vessel and gradually pull out of the dock, see the waving of handkerchiefs, and watch the receding shore." She and Clara experienced seasickness for only a few days, but Mary, whom Ruth now called Mother, was sick the whole way.

When the ship docked at Castle Gardens in New York harbor three weeks later and they disembarked, Ruth was thrilled to hear her father's voice through the crowd on the dock, "There she is with her dear little face." James and Mary Thompson Saxton married as soon as they arrived at their new home in Manayunk, Pennsylvania, a manufacturing town near Philadelphia. Ruth said of her new mother, "She was a splendid housekeeper, neat and thrifty. She proved to be a good wife and mother, and my debt to her is great indeed."

Ruth and Clara immediately went to work in the cotton mill where James was employed. The young girls had to defend themselves against the other mill girls. One day Ruth's dress got caught in the rollers. She ripped her dress in order to avoid injury and then began to cry—not because of the danger she had narrowly escaped, but because her dress was ruined. One of the workmen consoled her, saying, "Don't cry. There is lots of new clothes in America."

The May family soon moved to Philadelphia, where James found another job. For four months Mary was bedridden with rheumatism, so the twelve-year-old girls did all the housework, cooking, and washing. When she recovered, the girls worked in other homes as live-in help. During this period Ruth saw her family only on Sundays and missed them terribly. James was the branch president in Philadelphia, and missionaries often visited the family. To Ruth, "The fact that they had come from Zion as missionaries made them look more like angels than men."

The May family's hard work and thrift finally paid off, for in July 1867, James felt they were ready to go to Zion. Their train trip from Philadelphia to North Platte, Nebraska, took nine days. An unexpected day's stay at Niagara Falls was for Ruth "a glorious treat." That contrasted to the night they spent on the Missouri River on a cattle boat, about which Ruth commented, "You may be sure there was bellowing a plenty, but what did that matter? We were on our way to Zion."

When the family arrived at North Platte, they were disappointed to find their departure for Utah delayed a month. Not only would the delay increase their chances of getting caught in snow, but it also meant having to stretch their meager resources another month. James had only enough money to buy one yoke of oxen but not a wagon. He found a man who had a wagon but only one yoke of oxen, so they teamed up, with James driving as his contribution for the use of the wagon. The combined families meant that fourteen men, women, and children had to put all their possessions in the one wagon for the trek to Salt Lake City with sixty other wagons. Since the family that owned the wagon had first rights to any remaining space on it, Ruth, then thirteen years old, had to walk nearly all the way to the valley. Luckily, other families occasionally offered her a ride, making room for her in their already crowded wagons. With a strong sense of adventure, Ruth later wrote:

"One crack of [the captain's] whip on the tent or wagon

cover, whether at 3 a.m. or 5 a.m. meant 'roll out.' Killing snakes, plodding through the burning sands, wading streams, climbing mountains with sometimes an Indian scare, a threatened food shortage, sickness, sore feet, and a snow storm at South Pass, which detained us two or three days, were trifles. . . . But withal we could still sing:

> *"We may get wet a little*
> *When we have a shower of rain;*
> *The heat may skin our noses,*
> *But they'll soon get well again;*
> *And when we think of Zion's land*
> *We'll forget the wet and pain.*
> *So get up my lads, gee, whoa,*
> *Push on, my lads, hi, ho,*
> *For there's none can lead a life*
> *Like we merry Mormons do."*

At the Sweetwater River in Wyoming, Ruth thought that the willow and cherry trees lining the banks of the river, with the valley opening out beyond, were the most beautiful sight she had ever beheld. Ahead was Independence Rock, a granite landmark on which passers-by often painted or chiseled their names or messages for those to follow. Though she was tired, she eagerly climbed the rock and chiseled her name: *Ruth May, 1867.*[2] From the top of the rock, she could see to the east the route they had traveled and to the west the one they had yet to travel.

The Mays reached the valley in October 1867, getting their first glimpse of the valley desert at twilight. Ruth's first response was, "Did we come all this way for that?" Then, she later said, "This, however, was my first and last disappointment." The next morning the family attended general conference in the not-quite-completed tabernacle. A few days later James found a job as a carder in one of Brigham Young's businesses, the Deseret Woolen Mill, at the mouth of Parley's Canyon about eight miles from downtown Salt Lake City. They found a home to rent but had to crowd into one room of the two-room dwelling until the occupant of the other room could relocate. After only six months' attendance at school, Ruth and Clara went to work in the same factory as their father so that the family could buy a home as soon as possible.

For Ruth, life was not all work and no play, for she claimed she "did not lack for amusement." She wrote: "We often gathered at Brother James Cummings' home, the largest one in the little village, to spend the evening in song, reading, dialogues, forfeit games, mock weddings, and even dancing to comb and jew's-harp music. Sometimes our family was invited to a dance at Mill Creek and reminded to bring a candle along. Neither heat nor cold, dust nor mud mattered. Crossing creeks on poles was one of the feats we had to learn to do."

When Ruth was sixteen, she and her father went to work at a mill in Ogden, forty miles north of Salt Lake City. Of this experience she said: "The work was not the all-important thing to me. A sixteen-year-old girl coming from the city into a little country district at that time created quite a stir among the male fraternity; beaus were plentiful, and I assure you I had a good time." After working at the mill for seven months, Ruth returned to Salt Lake City and attended school for four more months. Except for some correspondence courses she took later in her life and one English class at the University of Utah, this was the end of Ruth's formal education.

Marriage and Family Life

In 1872 Ruth met Jesse W. Fox, Jr., a surveyor. They were married May 8, 1873, at the Endowment House by President Daniel H. Wells, a member of the First Presidency. Ruth was then nineteen and Jesse twenty. Following the wedding, the newlyweds rode in an open carriage to Jesse's parents' home for a family celebration. He had had a special three-tiered wedding cake made for the occasion; it was decorated with two foxes and six little foxes to represent himself, Ruth, and their future children. His prediction was only half right, for they eventually had twelve children. Ruth brought with her all of her possessions in one small trunk and $1.50 in cash.

Though deeply in love, Ruth and Jesse, like all newlyweds, had to adjust to each other's style of living. At her father's home

Ruth had been accustomed to having three meals a day at regular times. Jesse, however, was more easygoing and wasn't punctual about meals. She said, "I had to discipline myself, which was not always easy as I had a quick temper and a strong sense of justice."

The couple lived with his family for six months, then moved into the home next door, where their first child, Jesse May, was born April 14, 1874. Shortly after Jesse's birth, the two homes were torn down and replaced by a larger one, where the extended family all lived together. During the next few years the family moved several times. In 1875, Jesse was called on a mission to New York; however, he was recalled three months later to help his father survey the Utah Southern Railway. A daughter, Eliza May, was born during his absence, on January 10, 1876, and was six weeks old when her father returned home. She died two years later. George James was born July 15, 1877, and Ruth Clare, August 22, 1879. While the first four Fox children were each born in a different home, the next eight were all born in the same home at 261 West Second South: Feramorz Young, September 28, 1881; Hyrum Lester, November 14, 1883; Esther Vida, December 30, 1885; Frank Harding, December 5, 1887; Lucy Beryl, January 5, 1890; Leonard Grant, February 25, 1892; Florence Marie, January 30, 1894; and Emmeline Blanche, September 14, 1896.

Ruth was a devoted mother, but she was also aware of her own shortcomings and constantly tried to improve, as this excerpt from her life story indicates: "Our children were as good as most and better than some. They had a normal dislike for home chores and an irrepressible fondness of play. They brought their friends to join in outdoor games and we often invited them to join us at the long table in our dining room, where there were places at first for eight and soon for twelve to fifteen. There was mischief always in process, and at times tempers flared. I can't blame my children too much for their quarrels, as I was myself quick with sharp words and could not always count ten when provoked. I had been brought up in the English tradition of family discipline and applied the flat of my hand or a switch when I thought it necessary. I improved in self-restraint through the years, or else grew weary of the continued and fruitless effort to impose on my children my own standards of conduct. Though my first children got more whippings, I don't see that they are any nearer perfection than those that came later and escaped with fewer and lighter punishments."

She was undoubtedly hard on herself in assessing her mothering skills, for her daughter Vida remembered how Ruth wove the gospel into everyday happenings. When she cooked, she would stop what she was doing and say to her children, "Isn't it wonderful that an angel came to the Prophet and brought him the Golden Plates?" She taught her children to work: the girls helped with housework, and the boys took care of the chickens, horses, and cows. Vida also remembered her mother's homemaking skills:

"One of my most vivid memories of mother is at the sewing machine, where she pedaled and hummed hymns constantly. She was a very good sewer. I remember some lovely things she made for me, and I also remember her staying up till one in the morning making a dress for me to wear to a Sunday School Dance. . . . Another vivid picture is mother on Saturday morning. She used to make dozens of pies on Saturday — she tried to make enough to last over Monday night dessert — but I think she had a hard time because everyone of us used to bring someone home to Sunday dinner. . . . We always had two kinds of pie so that we could take our choice. I used to take a little of each."[3]

Once Ruth's son George and a neighbor boy, after reading adventure stories, took their ponies and rifles and ran away from home. They were not found until late in the night. George's brother Feramorz (Fera) recalled the incident:

"I think some of us experienced the most touching and impressive family circle that evening in all our lifetime at home. Mother gathered us around the fireplace of the living room and proceeded in the most kindly way to express her regret that any of her children would wish to leave home. . . . In the most kindly way she said to George, her message undoubtedly being meant for all of us, that whenever he got ready to leave home, he would not have to sneak away. There were tears in the eyes of all as she said, 'Next time let me know; we'll have a good dinner before you leave; I'll get together a basket of good food, and I'll walk the first mile with you.' Later in the big bedroom where four or five of us slept in two beds George said, with choking voice, 'Gee, that was worse than a licking.' "[4]

Jesse provided well for his large family, and during the first twenty years of their marriage the Foxes prospered. They were able to add a second story to their home and made plans to build a three-story dream home. Jesse also owned a farm located on the west side of the valley. Then in 1888, without consulting Ruth, he married a second wife, Rosemary Johnson. Five years later, during the Panic of 1893, he lost his dry goods business and eventually their home. Overcome with shock and depression, he went to bed for several days. Ruth handled the failure with equanimity. Until she married Jesse, she had known only humble circumstances, and her nature was such that she overcame sorrow and disappointment quickly. Although she said her heart was heavy, she tried to make the best of their circumstances and even hummed as she worked around the home. This irritated Jesse, who said, "By the great horn spoon, Polly, how can you sing at a time like this?"

Adjusting to their new circumstances, Ruth dismissed her hired help, gave increased responsibilities to her children, and rented out rooms. Jesse did not lose the farm, so the Foxes always had sufficient food to eat. Ruth felt they were comparatively well off, for she saw numerous people, including families, waiting in long lines for free soup and bread at a soup kitchen near their home. Earlier, in a patriarchal blessing from John Smith, the presiding patriarch, she had been told: "It shall be thy lot to feed the hungry and administer to the wants of the afflicted." The Fox home on West Second South was near the railroad depot, and many hungry, unemployed men knocked at Ruth's home to ask for food. "There must have been a mark on our front gate," she recalled, "for scarcely a week passed in those dismal days when some man did not ask for food. No one was ever turned away from the door, and it was not uncommon to see two and occasionally three at one time eating in our kitchen." Ruth invited one elderly man, who had no family in Utah, to live in the quarters of their former hired hand and fed him in exchange for odd jobs which, she said, she gave him "to remove the bitter taste of outright charity." Another woman, whose family left her when she joined the Church and who had been Ruth's laundry help, came to Ruth's home and told her, "Polly, I've come to stay until I die." Ruth took care of her until she died several months later.

When her son Fera became ill and could not do much physical labor, Ruth bought (with money raised by Jesse) a run-down rooming house for him to manage. She described purchasing "everything in the place, including bed-bugs, cockroaches, and roomers for less than $300.00." Several family members, including Ruth, helped Fera by making beds, filling lamps, emptying slop jars, and sweeping.

Ruth sorrowed deeply when her youngest daughter, Emmeline, died in 1914 of scarlet fever at age fourteen. Two years later her father suffered a debilitating stroke. So that she could be close to him during the day, she rented a home for him and for herself near the YLMIA offices, where she obtained work as a typist. She and Jesse no longer lived together, since he had a home with his second wife, but she took care of him during his two serious illnesses, the second one resulting in his death on December 12, 1928.

Illnesses and deaths in her family and financial losses and hardships caused Ruth to sum up her adversities philosophically: "Life brings some hard lessons. The sturdiest plants are not grown under glass, and strength of character is not derived from the avoidance of problems."

Personal Growth and Service to Others

Intermixed with raising her large family, running her home, and working at the YLMIA offices, Ruth was highly involved in community activities and church callings. She also wrote poetry and prose. From her childhood on, she loved to recite and write poetry. At age fifteen she wrote a poem about the martyrdom of Joseph Smith. Throughout her life, she wrote poetry for self-expression, to honor friends on special occasions, and to offer condolences. Her poetry began appearing in print in 1891, making her eligible to join the Press Club, a women's literary organization. She later was elected president. In 1923 the YLMIA general board published *May Blossoms,* a volume of her poems.

Ruth was also a member of the Reapers' Club, organized by Emmeline B. Wells for the "social and intellectual development" of women. Acutely aware of her limited schooling, she taught herself by reading, taking home-study courses, and observing language spoken by educated people. Sister Wells, fifth general president of the Relief Society and editor of the *Woman's Exponent*, had an enormous effect on Ruth's life. "No other woman had so great an influence as she in shaping my life," said Ruth. "I became her devoted disciple and she in turn loved me as a daughter. I named after her my last child, Emmeline Blanche, born September 14, 1896, when Sister Wells was the center of my orbit of public activities. For many years subsequently she had much to do with my progress."

Following Emmeline's example, Ruth became active in the woman's suffrage movement. Although women in Utah had had the right to vote since 1870, the passage of the Edmunds-Tucker Law by the U.S. Congress in 1886 rescinded those rights. When the Utah Territorial Woman Suffrage Association was organized in 1893, Emmeline became president and Ruth, treasurer. They had the opportunity to meet Susan B. Anthony when the national suffrage leader came to Utah to speak.

While most of the women working for suffrage were Democrats, Emmeline declared herself a Republican, as did Ruth, in direct opposition to her husband, Jesse, a staunch Democrat. The peak of Ruth's political activity was the year 1895, when she helped campaign for the ratification of the Utah State constitution, which included suffrage for women.

As chairman of the Ladies' Republican Club in Salt Lake City, Ruth helped organize similar clubs throughout the territory. When she and Emmeline traveled to Brigham City to organize a club, they were met at the depot with a salute of cannons. After Utah became a state in 1896, the first governor, Heber M. Wells, appointed Ruth to the board of the Deseret Agricultural and Manufacturing Society, on which she served for eight years.

Ruth received her first Church calling at age seventeen when Bishop George H. Taylor of the Fourteenth Ward called her to teach Sunday School. When the Fourteenth Ward Primary was organized in 1879, the president, Clara C. Cannon, selected

Ruth as her first counselor, a position she held for the next
nineteen years under three presidents.

In 1895 she was called as president of the ward YLMIA, a
position she held for three years simultaneously with her Primary calling. She was released from Primary in 1898 when she
was appointed to the YLMIA general board, but continued to
serve as ward YLMIA president until 1904. Of her calling to the
general board, Ruth said, "Thus began the most important
Church responsibility of my entire life, a calling that was to
continue for thirty-nine years, and that would give me opportunity for growth and service far beyond my fondest dreams."
In 1902, she also became a guide on Temple Square, serving
until 1929, when she became the YLMIA general president.

From the time Ruth was a young girl, she had been taught
to respect the priesthood. She described her attitude toward
Church leaders as "reverential." When she was called to the
general board, she found she "was much too self-effacing for
[her] own good," and she missed an important assignment because of it. She was scheduled to attend an MIA conference in
Rexburg, Idaho, following stake conference and the cornerstone-
laying of Ricks College. She rode to Rexburg on the same train
as President Joseph F. Smith and Elders George Q. Cannon,
Rudger Clawson, and Seymour B. Young. But, she said, "Being
the only woman and lacking nerve to invite the attention of the
brethren, I kept pretty much to myself on the over-night train
ride." When the train stopped at Idaho Falls, many Saints greeted
it with flags and flowers. Ruth was embarrassed when President
Smith told someone to give her some flowers because "she's a
good . . . worker." In Rexburg she again held back and let the
Brethren go with the crowds. She asked directions to the home
of Sister Ricks, the YLMIA president, and a man who was going
that way gave her a ride in his buggy. She was puzzled when
she found no one at home. Then she heard singing some distance
away. She walked toward the sound and found that a meeting
was in session at an open-air bowery. It was the MIA conference
she had come to attend. The meeting had been worked in
between the stake conference sessions to avoid conflict with a
circus coming to town, and she had missed it! "The breth-

ren . . . never let me get out of their sight again until we reached home," she said.

Carrying On

When the YLMIA was reorganized in April 1905, following the death of Elmina S. Taylor, Martha Horne Tingey was called to serve as president and Ruth May Fox became her first counselor. They served together for twenty-four years. Martha was released on March 28, 1929, because of ill health, and Ruth was called to be the general president. Since she was then seventy-five years old, she was somewhat surprised at the call. She mentioned her concern to President Heber J. Grant, and he handed her the following poem:

> *Age is a quality of mind;*
> *If your dreams you've left behind,*
> *If hope is cold;*
> *If you no longer look ahead,*
> *If your ambition's fires are dead —*
> *Then you are old.*
>
> *But if from life you take the best,*
> *And if in life you keep the zest,*
> *If love you hold;*
> *No matter how the years go by,*
> *No matter how the birthdays fly —*
> *You are not old.*

Ruth chose Lucy Grant Cannon as first counselor, Clarissa A. Beesley as second counselor, and Elsie Hogan as secretary. When President Grant set Ruth apart as YLMIA president, he blessed her that she would have "the same vigor of body and of mind in the future" that she enjoyed in the past and "great joy, peace and happiness."

At Ruth's first June Conference in 1929, two announcements were made: a summer camping program for all MIA girls and the merging of the *Young Woman's Journal* with the *Improvement Era,* beginning with the November issue. That October a stock market crash sent the United States into what became known as the Great Depression. Ruth, vividly remembering the Panic of 1893, resolved to help strengthen young girls and women for the coming economic adversity.

The year 1930 saw the centennial celebration of the organization of The Church of Jesus Christ of Latter-day Saints. That year the YLMIA and YMMIA chose as their June Conference theme "Onward with Mormon Ideals," suggesting that young people build on the foundations laid by their ancestors and carry on the work of the Church. That idea took root in Ruth's mind, and she wrote the words to a new anthem, titled "Carry On," which Alfred M. Durham set to music:

> *Firm as the mountains around us,*
> *Stalwart and brave we stand*
> *On the rock our fathers planted*
> *For us in this goodly land—*
> *The rock of honor and virtue,*
> *Of faith in the living God.*
> *They raised his banner triumphant—*
> *Over the desert sod.*

> Chorus
> *And we hear the desert singing:*
> *Carry on, carry on, carry on!*
> *Hills and vales and mountains ringing:*
> *Carry on, carry on, carry on!*
> *Holding aloft our colors,*
> *We march in the glorious dawn.*
> *O youth of the noble birthright,*
> *Carry on, carry on, carry on!*

> *We'll build on the rock they planted*
> *A palace to the King.*
> *Into its shining corridors,*
> *Our songs of praise we'll bring,*
> *For the heritage they left us,*
> *Not of gold or of worldly wealth,*
> *But a blessing everlasting*
> *Of love and joy and health.*

At the Sunday evening session of conference on June 8, the main floor of the Tabernacle was filled with young people who sang "Carry On," and when they reached the climax of the chorus, they waved gold and green programs. Ruth commented, "To say I was thrilled to hear an army of young men and women vocalizing the pledge to continue the work of their noble fathers is to express my feelings mildly."

The Lion House, which Brigham Young had built for his wives and children, housed the LDS High School until 1931, when it was turned over to the YLMIA as a social and learning center where young women could attend book reviews and classes in writing, speech, charm, and religion. In 1934 the YLMIA was renamed the Young Women's Mutual Improvement Association (YWMIA) to parallel the name of the young men's organization, the Young Men's Mutual Improvement Association.

The traveling libraries that Ruth helped organize as a board member in 1898 continued throughout her administration and increased to more than three thousand volumes. She felt that an organization dedicated to personal improvement should provide worthwhile reading materials for its members. Stake MIAs had the responsibility of purchasing and circulating books among the wards. Later, when public and school libraries were well established, the YLMIA discontinued the traveling libraries and began publishing lists of recommended books for its members.

When Ruth became president of her ward young women's organization in 1895, the YLMIA churchwide had 15,000 members in 400 wards. When she was released as general president in 1937, there were 70,000 YWMIA members in 1,000 wards, illustrating, as Ruth said, "the nature and magnitude of the task of the general officers and boards in planning lesson work and other activities for this immense organization and in providing necessary overall supervision and direction." The general officers' contact with local members and officers came mainly through the annual June Conference and visits to stake conferences. Ruth noted that she visited "most, if not all, of the stakes of Zion, including those in Canada, Mexico, and Hawaii." She and Albert E. Bowen, the YMMIA superintendent, conducted the first auxiliary conference held outside the continental United States, in Hawaii in 1935. One of Ruth's co-workers remarked that after a lengthy and arduous trip to visit stakes, she (the co-worker) often had to rest in bed for a day. "Well, maybe someday I'll come to that," responded Ruth, who was twenty-seven years older than her colleague.

Ruth's creativity and keen memory never dwindled as she grew older. On one occasion when the combined YWMIA and YMMIA presidencies hosted a dinner honoring Mutual workers, she recited a lengthy poem. After she sat down, a man sitting next to her said, "I would like a copy of that poem." She responded, "I'm sorry I don't have a copy I can give you; I made it up just now."[5]

Once the Music Committee, under the chairmanship of Ruth Hardy Funk and Roy M. Darley, asked Ruth to write another song that would have the stirring effect of "Carry On." She wrote lyrics and gave them to Crawford Gates to set to music. He lost the words, and when Sister Funk apologized to Ruth for the loss, she said, "Don't worry about that," and then repeated the words of "In Triumph We Shall Sing" from memory.[6]

In 1937 Ruth traveled to England with her daughter Vida Fox Clawson for the centenary of the British Mission. Sailing on the same ship were President Heber J. Grant and his counselor, J. Reuben Clark, Jr. President Grant asked Ruth to speak at several of the meetings in Lancashire and Preston. For Ruth, the highlight of the trip was a meeting attended by five hundred Saints on the banks of the River Ribble in Preston, where the first baptisms in the British Isles had taken place one hundred years earlier. When Ruth bore her testimony, according to Amy Brown Lyman, who was then serving as president of the auxiliaries in the European Mission, "she gave such an eloquent and stirring address that it thrilled the souls and touched the hearts of all of us who had the good fortune to be in attendance, and brought tears to the eyes of many." Ruth characterized the experience as "the crowning event in my long life of Church service."

Ruth had her first hospital stay at age eighty-two. A few years later, when she tripped on a rug and broke her hip, her family got her a wheelchair, but she used it very little and gave it to someone else who she felt needed it more than she did.

Release and Twenty More Years

As Ruth's eighty-fourth birthday approached, she seriously considered asking for a release from the YWMIA, for she thought, "It seems hardly appropriate for a woman in her eighties to be head of an organization emphasizing the word *young* in its title." She wrote to President Heber J. Grant, not asking for a release but indicating she would accept whatever decision the Brethren made. Just a few days before her birthday, on November 3, 1937, President Grant extended a release to her and her counselors and board. Asked by the new president, Lucy Grant Cannon, to address members of the outgoing board, Ruth expressed her love and assured them that she would live up to the promise given in her patriarchal blessing decades earlier that her last days would be her best days.

Ruth enjoyed twenty more years and filled her life with meaningful experiences. She became more involved in Relief Society and Gospel Doctrine classes, attended the temple regularly, and frequently spoke at MIA and fireside groups until her vision and hearing began to fail. She immersed herself in learning Braille but found she was happier and more successful in learning through a talking-book machine. She claimed she read more after she turned eighty-four than before. She also spent much of her time with her ever-growing family. President Grant, in his last few years, took a daily excursion in his car with his wife and usually invited two or three homebound widows, often including Ruth, to accompany them.

When her oldest son, Jesse, turned fifty, she gave him a family dinner, and as each of her remaining ten children reached that age, she held similar parties. In turn, Ruth's birthdays were celebrated enthusiastically by her family and friends. When she turned one hundred in 1953, the YWMIA honored her at a reception at the Beehive House during June Conference. She found that the older she got, the more she became a celebrity in the community. She wryly noted, "I am sure I would have missed much of my local importance had I arrived in Salt Lake two years after instead of two years before the completion of the railroad. Being a pre-railroad pioneer would alone have brought me some notice on special anniversaries, but only my long years of service in MIA could have opened the doors of the famous Beehive House for four grand birthday celebrations." These four celebrations, honoring her on her eighty-fifth, nine-tieth, ninety-fifth, and one hundredth birthdays, were attended by members of the First Presidency, the Council of the Twelve, and other Church leaders, city and state officials, and family and friends. Ruth commented, "That I deserve such honor is hard to understand."

Ruth continued to bear strong testimony. "Ever since I could understand, the gospel has meant everything to me," she said. "It has been my very breath, my mantle of protection against temptation, my consolation in sorrow, my joy and glory through-out all my days, and my hope of eternal life. 'The Kingdom of God or nothing' has been my motto."

When Ruth consulted a doctor about what she described as an "occasional feeling of faintness," he suggested that she drink a cup of coffee every morning. That advice did not set well with her. "I was ninety-two years of age," she commented, "and had by precept and example taught the importance of the 'Word of Wisdom' to my children and grandchildren, and in public addresses to thousands of Church members. I decided that living a few more years was not nearly as important as my example to posterity, and I have not followed the doctor's pre-scription." A week before she died, she asked her daughter Florence, with whom she was living, "Isn't this Fast Day? You'll be sure to pay my tithing, won't you?"

Ruth May Fox died April 12, 1958, at the age of one hundred and four. At her funeral on April 15, President J. Reuben Clark of the First Presidency and Clarissa A. Beesley, her counselor in the YWMIA, spoke, and seventy-five of her grandchildren and great-grandchildren sang "Carry On."

Ruth May Fox served the young women of the Church for nearly four decades as a member of the general board, as a counselor in the general presidency, and as the general presi-dent. Throughout a century of living, she never wavered from the principles she believed in and her unquestioning faith in the gospel of Jesus Christ. She credited her experiences (which she said were "far beyond my fondest dreams") and her youth and vigor to the Lord, who, she said, "has always done better for me than I could have done for myself."[7]

4

Lucy Grant Cannon
1937–1948

May I help you?" Lucy Grant Cannon asked a frantic young mother at the Union Pacific depot in Salt Lake City.

"My train isn't leaving for another twelve hours, and I have no place to go," answered the woman, who was holding a crying baby while a screaming toddler tugged at her dress.

"Come, I'll take you home," said Lucy.

Once home, Lucy fed the little family and then encouraged the mother to take a nap. While the woman slept, Lucy gave the children a bath and washed their clothes. Later that afternoon, she took the rested, happier family back to the train depot.[1]

This incident is typical of Lucy's compassion toward others and her genuine goodness. "I don't know how else you would describe my mother," remembers George Ivins Cannon, Lucy's son. "She was just a *good* woman. I can remember her saying, 'I may not be brilliant, but I can be good.' And she was."[2]

"The Blessing of Faith"

Lucy was born October 22, 1880, in Salt Lake City, the second daughter of Heber J. Grant, who later became the seventh president of The Church of Jesus Christ of Latter-day Saints, and Lucy Stringham.

In the spring of 1881, six-month-old Lucy developed whooping cough and soon lay near death. After her frantic parents had done all they could do, her father called John Rowberry, their stake patriarch, to give the dying baby a blessing. In this blessing Patriarch Rowberry said: "I seal upon thee the blessing of life and strength to thy body that thou shalt grow up to perfection in all of thy parts and become a mother in Israel in due time, and the Spirit of the Most High shall rest upon thee. Thou shalt bear in mind the instructions of thy mother and appreciate the counsel and blessing of thy father and I seal upon thee the blessing of faith to be healed when thou art sick and rebuke the disease that is now preying upon thee. Thou shalt receive strength and animation to thy lungs. Thou shalt be healed of this affliction."[3] This blessing was fulfilled, for Lucy recovered from the illness that nearly claimed her life. Yet there would be other times when she would need to call upon her faith to be healed, including a second encounter with death.

When Lucy was two years old, her father was called on October 16, 1882, to serve as a member of the Church's Quorum of the Twelve Apostles. Lucy, nicknamed "Lutie" by her immediate family and a few close friends to avoid confusion between her and her mother, enjoyed the advantages of being part of a prominent Salt Lake City family at the turn of the century. Her father, an astute businessman in banking, insurance, and business, used this background for the benefit of the Church.

The Grant family lived in the Salt Lake City Thirteenth Ward — the same ward in which her parents had grown up. Heber and Lucy, who had been married on November 1, 1877, eventually became the parents of six children: Susan Rachel, Lucy, Florence, Edith, Anna, and Heber, their only son, who died at age seven. During this time of plural marriage, the Grant family continued to grow as Heber married Huldah Augusta Winters on May 26, 1884, and Emily Harris Wells the next day. Augusta became the mother of one daughter, Mary. Five children were born to Emily: Martha Deseret (Dessie), Grace, Daniel Wells (who died at age four), Emily, and Frances.

"We were a large family — all girls," Frances later recalled. "There had been two boys, both of whom had died in childhood, whereas ten girls survived."[4] These ten girls formed the core of the family. "I always felt that there couldn't have been ten sisters who loved each other more than these ten sisters," said Lucy's son George, who enjoyed his nine aunts and numerous cousins.[5] Harmony and fun abounded among the members of this large family. "I don't think any of us felt that there was a differentiation between us," added Stan, another of Lucy's sons. "We were just as likely to go into their home as they were to come into ours. We were just one big family."[6]

Heber, a gentle father, often said, "They will only be children once, and I want them to get as much pleasure as they can out of life as they go along."[7] One of the favorite activities of his children and grandchildren was taking afternoon rides with him. His car held six people, and he would not leave until it was full. He often invited widows and homebound individuals as well as family members and their friends on his afternoon excursions.

A Year of Tragedy

Major changes occurred in thirteen-year-old Lucy's life in 1893: her mother's death; her own near death from diphtheria; and a change of the family's life-style as a result of the financial Panic of 1893.

Lucy's mother had suffered with ill health for almost three years before her death on January 3, 1893, at age thirty-eight. Lucy had been aware of her mother's failing health over the years, but when her father called the children into the bedroom and told them that their mother was dying, she could not accept the situation. She pled with him to heal her mother and brought some consecrated oil from another room for him to use. After Heber blessed his wife and dedicated her to the Lord, young Lucy, distraught, ran from the house.

Heber prayed that the Lord would bless his daughter with peace. Unaware of her father's prayer for her, Lucy knelt down and prayed for her mother's health to return. "Instantly a voice, not an audible one, but one that seemed to speak to my whole being, said, 'In the death of your mother the will of the Lord will be done,' " Lucy later wrote of the experience. "Immediately I was a changed child. I felt reconciled and almost happy."[8] Her mother died a few hours later, and the peace that filled Lutie allowed her to comfort her younger brother.

Heber's mother, Rachel Ridgeway Ivins Grant, was living with the Grant family at the time of her daughter-in-law's death.

A placid, faithful woman who was both aged and deaf, Grand-mother Grant provided comfort to the grieving family. "What-ever comes it will all come out right in the end," she said.[9] Though Rachel and Lutie assumed many household responsi-bilities, Grandmother Grant needed additional help to care for the six children, whose ages ranged from fourteen to four. Everyone was grateful when Heber's second wife, Augusta, and her daughter, Mary, moved in with them to help care for the family.

"Lutie . . . appreciated the loving care of Augusta W. Grant," Mary Kimball later wrote. "It was said that one could not tell that these were not her own children so kind and considerate was she of their welfare."[10] Shortly after his wife's death, Heber took his three oldest daughters, Rachel, Lucy, and Florence, on a trip to Chicago, New York, Boston, and Washington, D.C., hoping to help them adjust to their mother's death. The younger children remained at home with Grandmother Grant and Aunt Augusta. While in Washington, D.C., Rachel and Lucy contracted diphtheria. Lucy's pulse-rate dropped to twenty-eight beats a minute, and the doctors thought she would die. Elder Grant wrote of the events that followed:

"I was kneeling supplicating the Lord to spare her [Lutie's] life, pleading with him not to allow the additional sorrow to come to me of one of my children dying while I was away from home. I was shedding bitter tears, when the inspiration came that if I would send out for President George Q. Cannon and Bishop Hiram B. Clawson, who were then in Washington [D.C.], they could rebuke the disease, and that my daughter would live. I thanked the Lord for this manifestation and shed tears of gratitude that my daughter's life was to be spared. . . . President Cannon in his prayer rebuked the destroyer and announced that Lutie would live to be a mother."[11]

Lucy was healed and was able to return to Utah with her father and sisters.

The Panic of 1893 greatly affected the Grant family. Heber, a successful banker, developer, and promoter before the panic, experienced a dramatic change in income. Debts immediately replaced luxuries. The family rallied around him, and those who were able went to work. As the oldest children, Rachel and Lucy helped assume the burden of the household chores and even some of the debts. They also helped out in their father's office. "It was the greatest satisfaction of our young lives to feel that we were helping him by caring for ourselves and in that way sharing his heavy burden of debt," Lucy recalled.[12]

Having their Grandmother Grant living with them gave the girls a greater sense of security and stability. Heber's widowed mother had raised him alone, supporting herself by working as a seamstress and taking in boarders. Originally from a well-to-do Eastern family, she lost her inheritance when she joined the Church. She gradually began to lose her hearing as a young woman, and by the time she was forty-six, she had become almost completely deaf. She lived a quiet but happy life. "One good thing about being deaf is that I don't have to hear the bad things," she claimed.[13] Every afternoon, she put on a starched white apron trimmed with lace and came downstairs to visit and eat dinner. Her immaculate rooms in the Grant home were a peaceful retreat for the girls, whom she taught to sew and cook. She and Lucy developed an especially close relationship during this time. Lucy, who often studied in her grandmother's room, may have developed some of her placid nature from their association. One of her school friends once said, "Calm, serene, untroubled — such adjectives must have been coined to describe Lutie. I was never very good at spelling after I met Lutie, for I invariably spelled 'tranquility' — 'tranqui-"lutie" ' — for that is the effect she produced."[14]

Aunt Augusta, a schoolteacher and a patron of the arts, brought culture, such as attending the symphony and plays, to the family. Music played an important part in the Grant home. When Lucy was unable to attend school for an entire school year due to ill health, she turned to music and books. The Grant daughters loved to sing. When Florence and Edith were in their teens, their father took them to one of the finest vocal teachers in the country for lessons. Though the teacher was primarily interested in operatic voices, he agreed to listen to each girl sing. Afterwards he said he had never heard sweeter voices, but he agreed to give lessons only to Edith, since she was the one with an operatic voice. However, Lucy often sang with Florence at church, social functions, and funerals. She also played the piano, as did several of her sisters.

Nasturtiums, Marriage, and Family

George Jenkins Cannon loved Lucy from the first time he saw her in the classrooms of LDS High School. A son of Abraham Cannon, a member of the Quorum of the Twelve Apostles, and the oldest grandson of George Q. Cannon, the man who had blessed twelve-year-old Lucy in Washington, D.C., when she suffered from diphtheria, George grew up on a farm in southwest Salt Lake City near the Jordan River.

At fourteen, George often gathered bouquets of nasturtiums from his Grandfather Cannon's greenhouse, took them to school, and left them on Lucy's desk. When Lucy found the flowers, she would ask her best friend Grace Cannon, who was George's aunt, "Who put those flowers on my desk?" Grace would smile and say, "George did, of course." Lucy would smell the flowers and say, "Oh, he's so bashful. Why can't he give them to me instead of running away?"[15]

Though most of their courting was done as part of a large group, George and Lucy eventually began to date, but often as a threesome — George, Lucy, and George's best friend, Tracy Y. Cannon, who helped George carry on the conversation. This continued until George went on his mission. "When others saw him talking to mother after he received his mission call," said Jean Cannon Willis, Lucy's daughter, "everybody thought that he was asking her to wait for him. But he was only asking if he could write to her. He was too shy to ask for a commitment."[16]

The couple corresponded while George served a mission in Germany. He received quite a surprise when he returned home, for Lucy had been called as one of the first single women in the Church to serve a full-time mission. Before she left, he asked her to marry him after her mission, and she accepted. She served in the Western States Mission, headquartered in Denver.

Lucy returned from her mission in April 1902, and she and George were married in the Salt Lake Temple on June 26. At their outdoor wedding reception, the newlyweds stood on a small second-floor balcony while the Tabernacle Choir (of which Lucy was a member) serenaded them.

For most of their married life, Lucy and George lived with and cared for other family members. This pattern began immediately, for they moved in with Grandmother Grant to help care for her and for Lucy's three younger sisters—Florence, Edith, and Anna—while Elder Grant and his wife Augusta went to Japan to open the Japanese Mission. After they returned, George and Lucy moved into a home of their own and invited Grandmother Grant to come live with them. They cared for her until her death on January 27, 1909, seven years later.

Elder Grant took his wife Emily and three of her daughters—Dessie, Emily, and Frances—with him to England when he was called to preside over the European Mission. Upon their return, he built Emily her "dream house," but she was able to live in it only briefly. She died of cancer on May 25, 1908.

In 1918, after the death of her husband, George's mother moved in with the Cannons. Once again Lucy and her family willingly made room for an elderly relative; Grandmother Cannon lived with them for twenty-three years.

Continuing the close ties they had developed as children, Lucy and her sisters chose to live near each other as adults. Three members of the Grant family lived next door to each other in Salt Lake City—Heber J. Grant on the corner of "A" Street and Second Avenue, his daughter Florence Smith and her family next door to him, and Lucy Cannon next to Florence. Others of the ten sisters—Mary, Rachel, Frances, Dessie, and Anna—lived nearby. Emily's grandson, Truman G. Madsen, enjoyed growing up in this neighborhood because the children "had refrigerator privileges in any of the aunts' houses."[17]

The gardens around George and Lucy's home always had nasturtiums blooming in the summer, and a nasturtium bouquet on the dining room table or mantle was a reminder of the days when bashful George had "wooed" Lucy anonymously with flowers in school.[18] George worked in the insurance business, eventually becoming executive vice-president of Beneficial Life Insurance Company. With no living sons, Heber J. Grant had a father-son relationship with his sons-in-law.

In a patriarchal blessing, Lucy was promised she would

have sons and daughters. Her first baby, Rachel, was born April 17, 1903, and Irene was born March 20, 1906. After Florence's birth January 16, 1909, the doctor told Lucy she should never have another baby. Lucy subsequently underwent several operations incident to childbearing before giving birth to another daughter, Jean, on June 17, 1917. She and George finally had a son, George Ivins, who was born March 9, 1920. But Lucy's blessing had promised *sons,* so she tried again. Her next baby was a daughter, Lucy Grant, born April 19, 1922. At last she gave birth to a second son, Heber Stanley, who was born June 20, 1925. Lucy felt that her blessing had been fulfilled.

Music, which had been a part of Lucy's life since her childhood, continued to be important to her and her family. The Cannons always had a grand piano and their children learned to play it. "I remember Mother singing early every morning while she did the washing down in the basement," George recalls. "We had a three-story house, including the basement, but we could hear her even up in the bedrooms. She was our alarm clock." Jean remembers that her mother used to have the children sing before they went to school every morning. "We listened to the opera every Saturday and the Philharmonic orchestra every Sunday," Stan says. And "Sunday evenings before we went to bed, we listened to 'The Spoken Word' broadcast from Temple Square."[19]

The Cannons had a cabin at Brighton in Big Cottonwood Canyon, east of Salt Lake City. Lucy used to take her children, their friends, and their cousins to the cabin for the summer months. In later years, after she was called to serve in the MIA, she would often sign award certificates and read the young women's manuals during those visits to the cabin.[20]

Caring for others always came naturally to Lucy. She welcomed those in need into her home, took food to the sick, remembered birthdays and other special occasions, and provided a listening ear and words of encouragement. She was a marvelous cook, according to her children. "We were always carting pea soup and breadsticks or candy to someone," remembers her son George. "That was our life, carrying food to anyone who was sick or lonely and then going out later to pick up the pots and pans."[21]

Lucy also showed her concern for others through the written word. Every Monday she layered onionskin paper with carbon paper until she had enough copies for every family member away from home, then rolled the papers into the carriage of a typewriter on a table in an alcove off her dining room. She began her letters with the words "Dear Grant Clan," and once or twice a day throughout the week, she would add a few lines of news or inspiration. Her daughter Jean has copies of most of the twenty-two hundred letters Lucy wrote.[22]

Lucy loved to entertain. After her father, Heber J. Grant, was sustained as president of the Church on November 23, 1918, he often asked Lucy and George to help him entertain. "From the alcove in my dining room I could look over into Aunt Lucy's dining room and see who she was entertaining," recalls Lucy's niece, Florence Smith Jacobsen, who became the sixth YWMIA general president. "Aunt Lucy often entertained General Authorities or other dignitaries for her father on general conference weekends. And all our big family birthday parties were held in Aunt Lucy's and Uncle George's basement. My cousins and I always served the food and had a wonderful time."[23]

Service in the YWMIA

At age eighteen, Lucy was called to be the president of the Thirteenth Ward YLMIA and began what would be twenty-five years of service with the young women. When she returned from her mission in 1902, she was called again to serve in the YLMIA. Over the next several years she was a member of ward and stake YLMIA presidencies.

Martha H. Tingey was YLMIA president when Lucy was called to the general board on October 8, 1916. Lucy was assigned to a committee to provide a program for sixteen- and seventeen-year-old girls, whom they called Intermediate Girls. By February 1922, there were seventy-one Intermediate groups with 1,011 girls in twenty-two stakes. On July 5, 1922, the name was changed to Junior Girls.

When it became necessary for President Tingey's second counselor, Mae Taylor Nystrom, to be released, Lucy was called to replace her on July 15, 1923. This presidency served against the historical backdrop of the lavish life-style of the "roaring twenties." A strong economy created a comfortable setting for many, with smoking and drinking becoming common in radio programs and motion pictures, and many people adopting a worldly way of life. Girls bobbed their hair, wore loose dresses, and were called "flappers." Among the precautions the new YLMIA presidency took to guide LDS girls was a four-year study designed to preview films and make recommendations.

Lucy willingly did whatever she could to help Sister Tingey and the other YLMIA leaders, and that included driving them around town. Her son George adds a humorous note to this subject: "Mother was such a tiny little lady that she couldn't see over the engine of the car. She had to look between the steering wheel and the hood in order to see."[24]

Her years of service on the general level of MIA coincided with her early years of motherhood. "The general board members were just like part of our family because they visited our home so often," Jean remembers, "but we never resented mother's church work or felt that she put it before us."[25] "Mother used to take my sister Lucy and me to her meetings," said Stan, "and we'd be in the back being tended and doing crafts. Sometimes she would involve us in doing little jobs so we felt like we were helping."[26] Lucy was especially close to Clarissa Beesley, whose niece Virginia married Stan Cannon.

June Conference was a time when all of Lucy's children were able to help her. Neighbors shared their flowers to decorate the stand in the Tabernacle, and the day before conference, the Cannon children would go around the neighborhood to gather the flowers, which they put into big tubs of water in the basement. The next morning, the entire family would load the flowers and baskets that they had saved throughout the year into the car and take them to the Tabernacle, where they arranged the bouquets right on the platform.

In March 1929 Martha Tingey was released as president of the YLMIA, and the new president, Ruth May Fox, selected Lucy as first counselor and Clarissa A. Beesley as second. That year George Cannon was also called to serve in a stake presidency. Elsie Talmage Brandley, in her *History of the YLMIA*, described Lucy during this period: "Deeply religious, unselfish, and obedient, she carries about her no atmosphere of sanctimony, but transmits the abundant faith which is hers into beautiful living, and demonstrates every day the loveliness of true and vital spirituality. Her goodness engenders in others a desire to do good. . . . To many girls in the MIA both now and in the years gone by, Sister Lucy Cannon stands as a light, illuminating the path that leads toward salvation. She is very good, very lovable, and very happy, harboring within her heart a love for all humanity, and unwavering assurance of the divinity of the gospel of Jesus Christ."[27]

At June Conference in 1929, the new presidency announced the merging of the *Young Woman's Journal* and the *Improvement Era*. When the first issue of the new *Improvement Era* was published in October, the YLMIA threw a "wedding party" complete with wedding cake to celebrate. However, a few days later the festive spirit was dampened when the stock market crashed with dire consequences for the entire nation. In contrast to the comfortable life-style of the 1920s, the depression years of the 1930s were filled with hard financial times for nearly everyone. All three members of the YLMIA presidency had lived through a similar depression during the Panic of 1893. Whenever they spoke, they shared their experiences and the solutions they had found at that time.

One of Lucy's major accomplishments during her twenty-five years in the general YLMIA presidency took place in 1930–1931: the renovation of the Lion House, which had been used as part of the LDS High School. She had the vision and the determination to make it a successful social and educational center for Salt Lake City. She even involved her younger children in the project — they grew sweet-potato vines in glass jars at home for the Lion House windowsills and helped their mother arrange the furniture. At the reopening celebration of the Lion House, Lucy's son George played the piano as the musical background.

In the book *History of the YWMIA,* Marba C. Josephson described the newly renovated building: "In addition to providing cafeteria privileges, [the home] provided rooms for social parties; restroom accommodations for girls and women; organized classes in dressmaking, handicrafts, literature, cooking, English, storytelling; a lunchroom where girls brought their lunches and enjoyed a brief period of relaxation during the midday; reading rooms; and interest through the restoration of one or two of the historic rooms to their original condition."[28]

During the following years, Lucy faced a painful personal challenge at home: her daughter Florence was dying from cancer. Lucy wrote the feelings of her heart in her weekly family letter: "A mother when she sees her offspring suffer would willingly change places, she feels she could bear it probably better because perchance she has suffered before, she has felt the pains of travail in bringing that child into the world, and she could bear the pain again and again for its sake. But Mary [the mother of Christ] did stand at the foot of the cross, and undoubtedly called upon her God for help for strength to witness that death struggle of her beloved son, and God did give her strength . . . and in that hour of suffering her soul was purified as suffering and sorrow can purify the soul. . . . And so in this way I talked to myself.

"This experience has been a hallowed one, I am a better woman from having passed through it. I feel more keenly for those who suffer. . . . I would not ask that I did not have this experience. I would not call my daughter back if I could. . . . Sorrow and joy two of the great factors that come into life to make it real have been experienced by us in having and losing this lovely daughter."[29] Florence died on March 19, 1933.

The following year, an important change for the young women's organization took place: the name Young Ladies' Mutual Improvement Association was changed to Young Women's Mutual Improvement Association.

President of the YWMIA

In October 1937, after serving together for more than eight years, Ruth May Fox and her counselors were released, and Lucy Grant Cannon, at age fifty-seven, became the new YWMIA president. Lucy's choice of counselors and executive secretary resulted in a diverse but strong presidency. First counselor Helen Spencer Williams, a granddaughter of Brigham Young, was a strong creative thinker and writer with the ability to communicate warmth and love to others, while second counselor Verna

Wright Goddard was a dynamic speaker, personal counselor, and problem solver. Clarissa Beesley became the executive secretary and organized the YWMIA office with businesslike efficiency. Six years later, on May 17, 1944, Helen Williams was released because of health problems; Verna Goddard became first counselor, and Lucy T. Anderson second counselor.

When Lucy Grant Cannon became YWMIA general president, the Great Depression still hung heavy over America and much of the world, and war loomed on the horizon. She was well aware of the difficulties facing her as leader of more than seventy-six thousand young women worldwide, but as a woman of faith, she accepted the challenge. During her administration, the YWMIA program grew strong. Each class had its own lesson manual, code, and symbol — the beehive for Beehive girls, the rose for the Junior class, and a sheaf of wheat for Gleaners. The Golden Gleaner award was established as the highest YWMIA award, and special interest groups, nicknamed "Spingro," were organized for adults over age twenty-three.

Against the backdrop of the depression and threat of war, members of the YLMIA found diversion in roadshows filled with music and dancing. The influence of this golden time of radio and movies carried over into the YLMIA programs, with talent numbers becoming part of the opening exercises. Quartets became popular, and the jitterbug was allowed at dances.

War became a reality for Americans on December 7, 1941, when Japanese planes bombed Pearl Harbor. The 1942 MIA theme reflected the times: "Be strong and of good courage; be not afraid, neither be thou dismayed; for the Lord thy God is with thee whithersoever thou goest." (Joshua 1:9.) With the war, young Latter-day Saints were affected by worldly influences such as cheek-to-cheek dancing; dark red lipstick and nail polish, bare legs, and "snood" netting over long hair for the girls; and, "Zoot suits" for the boys.[30] Standards were posted at the entrances of ward recreation halls for MIA activities, requesting appropriate dress, appropriate dancing, and adherence to the Word of Wisdom.

Leaders began to strongly emphasize the importance of a temple marriage in lessons, articles, talks, and yearly standards nights. At June Conference, a "Clean Life" program focused on moral purity. Signatures of young people who vowed to "attain cleanliness of thought" were collected from around the world, bound into four volumes, and presented to President Grant.[31]

The war took its toll in other areas. The 1944 Diamond Jubilee celebration was minimized with scaled-down activities. When paper shortages limited the publication of manuals, the general presidency and board began communicating with MIA leaders through the *Improvement Era*. Gas-rationing forced a reduction in travel for leaders on the general level and a curtailment of ward activities that required members to travel long distances. Since the number of young women in the wards greatly outnumbered the number of young men, the YWMIA dance committee came up with the idea of a "One for Two" dance — one boy dancing with two girls. It didn't catch on — but all-girl dances at dance festivals did.

During the war years, Lucy became aware that many young women and their mothers needed to go to work and many had to leave their hometowns to find work. The YWMIA organized a "Big Sister" program, where local leaders were counseled to take special interest in out-of-town girls. The Beehive House continued to be used as a residence for girls who came to Salt Lake City to find work.

On May 14, 1945, a few days after the war in Europe ended, Lucy's father, President Grant, died. In her newsletter of May 15, she told family members, "Altho tears stream down my cheeks as I write, they are not tears of grief for him, but tears of grief for those of us who have loved and lost a great and good father, grandfather, husband, and friend."[32]

Four months later, fighting ceased in the Pacific. After nearly four years of war, America was again at peace. The joyous spirit of peacetime was captured by three thousand dancers at a dance festival held at the Saltair resort on the shores of the Great Salt Lake the following June.

In 1947, Utah celebrated the one hundredth anniversary of the pioneers' entry into the Salt Lake Valley, and Lucy oversaw the celebration among more than 104,000 members of the YWMIA throughout the Church, with such events as square dancing, parades, and reenactments of the pioneer trek. This centennial focus contributed to a happy ending to Lucy Grant Cannon's administration.

After YWMIA

At general conference in April 1948, after serving as general president of YWMIA for ten and a half years, Lucy Grant Cannon was released.

Someone once asked Lucy what she would ask for if she had to live her life over again. "I would request better health," she reportedly answered.[33] Prior to her release from the YWMIA, she had begun to suffer from Meniere's Syndrome, an inner-ear disease that causes dizziness, and throughout her life she had many health problems. But she never complained; in fact, she loved life and truly enjoyed it. In her "retirement years" she continued to find ways to serve. For several years she tended her grandchildren so her daughter Jean could teach Primary. She still took food or candy to those in need, wrote letters to her extended family, enjoyed fine music and literature, and studied the scriptures. And as she began to wear out after a lifetime of service, others served and cared for her.

After George's death at eighty-five, on April 2, 1965, the Cannon children regularly cared for their mother. Irene and her husband, Tom Lloyd, moved in with Lucy, and the other children came on a regular basis to help with her care. Completely bedridden for the last six months of her life, she bore her illness with patience and often thanked those who cared for her. On May 28, 1966, she died at age eighty-five.

"Happiness comes from within; it is a state of mind," Lucy wrote in the *Young Woman's Journal* in a statement that seems to sum up her own life. "One has to have experience with sorrow and pain in order to feel happiness in joy and health. To gain experience is one of the great objects of life, and the way in which one accepts the various situations of life shows progress or retrogression."[34] Lucy found happiness as she accepted the challenges of her own life. Though she did not have vigorous health, she used her limited physical strength to serve the Lord, her family, and her friends. Her faith sustained her through personal challenges and in service to young women.

5

Bertha Stone Reeder

1948–1961

Visitors to Woodland, a mountain site near Kamas, Utah, that had been purchased for a girls' camp, had a difficult time appreciating its beauty and its possibilities. Lucy Harris, the YWMIA president in the Pioneer Stake, said, "It didn't look like much at the time, hot and dry." But when Bertha S. Reeder, YWMIA general president and an ardent camping enthusiast, began to describe the potential of the site, Lucy changed her mind and said, "Just hearing her pleasing voice made me visualize what it would be someday."[1]

Later, when young girls gathered around the campfires at Woodland on summer evenings, some of them had a difficult time appreciating their own strengths and possibilities. According to another YWMIA leader, when Bertha began speaking to the girls of their potential "in her gracious manner, she aroused in them the desire to live righteously and to be healthy, happy, wholesome children of God."[2]

Because of her personal graciousness, her radiant smile, and her firm faith in the gospel of Jesus Christ, Bertha Stone Reeder inspired many—her family, missionaries, co-workers, and young women and their leaders—to rise to their potential.

Ancestry and Childhood

Bertha's great-grandparents, William and Mary Cruse Stone, joined The Church of Jesus Christ of Latter-day Saints in Newberry, England. Mary's father, a wealthy landowner, owned a home with thirty-six rooms. Although Mary was married and had children at the time of her conversion, her parents disowned her and would have nothing more to do with her. The Stones left England and had traveled as far as Council Bluffs, Iowa, when William and Mary became too ill to go any farther. They permitted their fourteen-year-old daughter, Mary Eliza, to go on to Utah with a family of eight orphaned children whose wagon was driven by a deaf man. Trail life, cooking, washing, and caring for children were a surprise to Mary Eliza, who, because of her upper-class background, had never done any physical labor in her life.

Mary Eliza worked as a maid after she arrived in Utah, then married William Birch Hutchins when she was seventeen. Brigham Young sent the young couple to help colonize Slaterville in Weber County, some forty miles north of Salt Lake City. Mary Eliza and William had eleven children, of whom Bertha's mother, Esther Priscilla, was the fifth. Esther married Frederick Naper Gough Stone March 14, 1888, and they had four daughters and a son. Bertha Julia Stone, the second daughter, was born October 28, 1892, in Ogden, Utah. The first daughter, Olive, who was born in 1889, and the third daughter, Clarissa, born in 1894, both died as infants. The fourth daughter, Blanche, was born in 1896, and the only son, Leslie, was born in 1898.

Bertha's father worked for the streetcar company in Ogden. "When I was a little girl I loved ice cream," she wrote in her diary, "and there was an ice cream parlor at about 15th Street. . . . Dad used to take me on the streetcar and give me money for a dish of ice cream and leave me while he went to the end of his run, then picked me up on the way back."[3]

In 1900, when Bertha was eight years old, her father became a brakeman for the Southern Pacific Railroad and the family moved to Promontory, a remote town fifty miles northwest of Ogden. Their home was near the place where the last spike of the transcontinental railroad was driven on May 10, 1869. Only three Latter-day Saint families lived in Promontory, and sacrament meeting was held in the Stones' home. Esther taught Sunday School, which was attended by twenty children of various denominations.

Bertha vividly remembered a lesson her father taught her

on tithing. He gave a calf to the three children to raise. The calf, which they named Annie Rooney, followed them around and nuzzled against their legs. When they returned home one day from a visit to their grandmother, the children found that their father had sold their beloved pet to the butcher. Heartbroken, they sat around the table while Fred gave them each a third of the money from the calf. He told them, "Now the Lord gave you Annie Rooney, and you have to give back the Lord the tenth that he asked for." Three quarters of a century later Bertha recalled that experience and commented, "That was the first tithing I ever paid, and I've paid tithing ever since."[4]

When Bertha was twelve, the family moved back to Ogden. She was thrilled when her parents bought a new piano that had four pedals and a mandolin and guitar attachment. She loved music and her piano lessons and soon became proficient enough to serve as Sunday School organist. At fourteen, she became the ward organist, playing for Sunday School and sacrament meeting as well as Religion Class and Primary. At sixteen, she was called to serve as the stake Sunday School organist. Then the railroad transferred her father to Sparks, Nevada, where the family lived for a year. Bertha played the organ for the Methodist church in Sparks.

After graduating from high school in Ogden, Bertha attended the Weber Academy and served on the Sunday School stake board. She also taught piano lessons to twenty students. Later, while serving as a ward YLMIA president, she organized an orchestra to play for ward dances.

Marriage, Family, and Widowhood

When Bertha was nineteen, her mother died. Bertha took care of the family for a few months until her father hired a housekeeper, Ellen Smuin, whom he later married.

On August 10, 1912, two months before her twentieth birthday, Bertha was married to Christopher Aadnesen, who was thirteen years her senior. They settled in Ogden and had two children, a daughter, Oertel, born October 4, 1913, and a son, Grant C., born April 10, 1915. Christopher owned a sporting goods store and a drugstore and earned a comfortable living for his family. Both Bertha and Christopher enjoyed camping, hunting, and fishing, often with their children.

Bertha was a good shot and a fine fisherwoman. Oertel remembered the time her mother saw two sage hens go past their campground. She shot the hens with a gun and had them cleaned and cooked over an open fire before the men came back from hunting. They had shot nothing.[5] Grant described an experience when he was fly fishing in the Yellowstone River and his mother not only outcast him, but she also caught two fish to every one he caught.[6]

The Aadnesens also enjoyed traveling. One year they took off the day school was out in the spring and toured the Northwest and British Columbia, drove down the coast to Los Angeles, and then stopped in Las Vegas on the way home. They did not return until two weeks after school began in the fall.

Bertha was "Aunt Bertha" to Oertel's and Grant's friends. A warm and loving person, she enjoyed entertaining and was a wonderful cook. "Seldom did we have dinner alone, with just our family," said Oertel.[7] Grant noted that his friends and dates all liked to gather at his house because they felt so welcome. Charles E. Peterson, a friend of Oertel's, wrote of Bertha, "She was so warm and vibrant that her friendliness captivated me. It was always a joy to come to [her] home. I can still taste the chocolate cake and milk and sandwiches that we would have on Sunday evenings."[8]

Bertha presented a striking appearance, with her "startlingly black hair," Grant remembered. He characterized his mother as very refined, "a great lady."[9] Helena Larson Allen, who later served as Bertha's executive secretary, said, "Bertha had such an outgoing personality that within a minute or two of meeting someone, she was their friend. She had style—she was good looking and had such a lovely smile."[10]

According to Oertel, Bertha taught her children "to like people and to share everything. We had our own lives to live, and we were told to get an education even if we had to scrub floors."[11] She insisted that her children each learn to play a musical instrument. Grant played the violin and Oertel, the piano. Oertel also became an accomplished ballerina and had an opportunity at thirteen to dance with a company in New York City, but Bertha thought she was too young and refused to let her go.

During her early married years, Bertha served as a Sunday School teacher, Relief Society organist, president of the Ogden Eighth Ward YWMIA, and president of the Mount Ogden Stake Primary. She became involved with the Cub Scout program and helped organize it as part of the Primary program. Christopher was not a religious person, though he contributed generously to the Church and did not object to Bertha's activity.

Christopher died on October 21, 1930, as the result of an accident suffered while on a hunting trip. At thirty-six, Bertha had to adjust to widowhood; she was sealed in the temple to Christopher after his death. When Grant was called to serve a mission in Germany and Oertel left home to attend Utah State Agricultural College in Logan, Bertha was alone for the first time in her life.

On September 12, 1934, Bertha was married to William Henry Reeder, Jr., a widower with one son, William H. Reeder III. Bertha's husband was a municipal judge in Ogden, and she always called him "Judge," as did his friends and family. Bertha and Judge enjoyed fishing together. They also had a mutual interest in Church history and doctrine and had a library of 1,500 Church books, including first editions of the Book of Mormon and Doctrine and Covenants in every language in which they had been translated.

Presiding Over the New England Mission

In 1939, Bertha was called to the Primary general board, serving under general president May Green Hinckley. Two years later, Judge was called to preside over the New England States Mission, with headquarters in Cambridge, Massachusetts. When President David O. McKay of the First Presidency set Bertha apart as a missionary, he gave her a blessing in which he said: "We bless you that you may find happiness in your labors; that as you go forth among the people, strangers as well as members, you will radiate your characteristic cheerfulness and unwavering faith to the end that those who come within the radiation of your personality and your faith in the Gospel of Jesus Christ will be led to investigate the truth."[12] Bertha's six-and-a-half year service was marked by her friendliness and her faith.

Housing in the Boston area was scarce at the time because of World War II, so the missionaries all lived in the seventeen-room mission home, which the Church had recently purchased. The home, on Brattle Street in Cambridge, had belonged to Henry Wadsworth Longfellow's niece and was across the street from Longfellow's own home. The day after the Reeders moved in, a woman called on them and asked why the brass door knocker was green. Bertha discovered that not only was the door knocker made of brass, but all the hinges and doorknobs were also brass. She and several missionaries spent a day cleaning the brass with vinegar and salt, and they kept them polished from then on.[13] Another visitor, discovering that the Reeders did not have any pewter in the home, cried in astonishment, "Living in New England and no pewter?"[14]

As mission mother, Bertha cooked three meals a day for the missionaries and her husband. They frequently had guests, such as General Authorities and general Relief Society president Belle S. Spafford. Though at times meal preparation was a challenge because of wartime food rationing, their meals were "always superbly delicious," according to one missionary, Kenneth W. Porter. He remembered Bertha as a "prodigious worker" who kept up the large mission home with little outside help and who collected, cleaned, and mended clothing for the welfare program. "I have seen her so tired she almost dropped, but she never complained," he said. "This was all in addition to heading the Primary, Relief Society, and YWMIA programs."[15]

As leader of the auxiliaries, Bertha spent many hours adapting lesson manuals for the small mission branches. The Cambridge Branch Primary met on Sunday morning at the same time as the priesthood, and from a small group of eight children, membership increased to forty-five. Every Sunday evening the Reeders hosted a fireside at the mission home for the servicemen stationed nearby. As many as seventy people, including non-members, attended the firesides, which were taught by George Albert Smith, Jr. Bertha commented, "We converted quite a few people through that Sunday night service."[16]

Part of the Reeders' time in the mission field was spent

visiting and helping outlying branches of the mission, which extended into the Maritime Provinces of Canada. "We tried to make them all as near like a branch of the Church or a ward as possible because we had to develop leadership," Bertha said. "So we put in a chorister and an organist and organized [each branch] just about like a ward, and tried to have [the members] realize what their responsibilities were. Our hardest job was teaching them the responsibilities and the organization of the Church because they didn't understand it. [The new converts] had been used to going and sitting and listening. Now they had to be leaders. We had to follow it up really closely to develop this leadership."[17] By the conclusion of their mission, the Reeders had every branch functioning under local leadership.

The Reeders returned to Utah in May 1947, in time for the dedication of the "This Is the Place Monument," which Judge had been instrumental in erecting as vice-chairman of the monument committee. While in New England, he had frequently checked on the monument, which was cast in bronze in New York City. Bertha remembers watching the "monument grow from eighteen inches to seventeen feet."[18]

General President of the YWMIA

In April 1948, eleven months after the Reeders returned home, President George Albert Smith called Bertha to serve as the fifth general president of the YWMIA. Because she had served on the Primary general board, she was surprised to be called to serve in MIA. When she told President Smith that she felt she didn't know enough about the young women's organization, he replied, "Sister Reeder, if I thought you thought you did, we would not have called you."[19] She slept very little for several nights after that meeting, and to keep her mind off the tremendous responsibility that was now hers, she laundered everything in her home.

Bertha was sustained at general conference on April 6, but it wasn't until May that she chose her counselors: Emily Higgs Bennett, first counselor, and LaRue Carr Longden, second counselor. The presidency began their service after June Conference. In the interim, they met with outgoing president Lucy Grant

Cannon and her board, thus making the transition smooth. Sixty women were called to serve on Bertha's general board.

Shortly after she became YWMIA president, Bertha and Judge moved to Salt Lake City so she could be closer to Church headquarters. Judge worked in Salt Lake City as legal counsel for Zion's Securities Corporation.

At the time Bertha became president, all girls were enrolled not only in YWMIA, but also in a girls' program that correlated with the Aaronic Priesthood program for the boys and was under the direction of the Presiding Bishopric. The girls' program, which originated in Salt Lake City's Granite Stake in 1940 and was adopted for the whole church in 1946, was carried out in each ward under a chairwoman with two assistants. The aims of the program were to encourage girls to attend church meetings, pay a full tithe, observe the Word of Wisdom, give at least one talk each year, and participate in an annual welfare project. Bertha, who felt that the girls' program conflicted with the YWMIA program, asked the First Presidency if both programs could be coordinated under the YWMIA. Within the first year of her presidency, the new coordinated program was introduced in several stakes, and in 1950 it was adopted for the Church. Each girl who attended 75 percent of sacrament, Sunday School, and YWMIA meetings qualified to receive an Individual Award. An attendance secretary was called to serve in each ward as a member of the YWMIA board. Bertha felt that by recording attendance at all three meetings, not only would participation by young women increase, but also leaders would be better able to know where the members were and to seek out those who were not attending.

The new presidency realigned the age groups, changing the Beehive department from three years to two, for twelve- and thirteen-year-old girls; creating the Mia Maid department for fourteen- and fifteen-year-olds; and dividing the Gleaners into Junior Gleaners (in 1959 the name was changed to Laurels) for sixteen- and seventeen-year-olds, and Gleaners for young women who were eighteen through twenty-four.

In 1949 the combined YWMIA and YMMIA published the first issue of the *Leader,* a monthly bulletin sent to stake leaders containing messages, articles, and information concerning each department in the MIA programs. The following year the first stake speech festivals were held and the first honorary Golden Gleaner awards were given. Bertha and her counselors changed the name and focus of the former "recreation department," with the new sports committee stressing increased physical activity. Interstake sports competitions began in 1952.

Bertha's love of the outdoors carried over to the YWMIA. "It is our desire that every young woman have a camping experience," she said.[20] She organized a camp committee on the general board and urged all stakes to purchase camp sites. A purist, she believed that camping should be done in sleeping bags and tents, and she disdained "dude camping" — sleeping in lodges or cabins. She visited many camps in the Church and helped stakes organize their camp programs. In an article published in the *Improvement Era,* she expressed her philosophy:

"Nature does indeed renew those who keep close to her. Nowadays in the speed of our communication, with airplanes, automobiles, radio, and television, we seem to be crowded close upon each other. Even in rural areas, urban ideas have crowded until we have little real communion with nature.

"If I were in my teens, I would take time to come close to nature. I would learn to fish, to swim, to hike, and to find joy in God's great out-of-doors. I would learn to listen to the earth noises — to hear the birds, the crickets, the sighing of the wind in the trees, the lapping of the water against the shore. I would learn to see the differences in trees, in flowers, in grasses. I would realize again more fully the infinite variety in God's creation. I would learn to feel the difference in the seasons and to love each for what it gives to me. I would know that rain and sunshine are both important in God's plan."[21]

Each year thousands of ward and stake MIA leaders gathered in Salt Lake City for the annual June Conference to receive instruction and inspiration for the coming year. In addition to instructional sessions, music, drama, dance, and speech festivals showcased the work of the MIA and gave young people opportunities to participate in large productions. The dance festivals, with thousands of participants, were held at the University of Utah stadium in Salt Lake City. The threat of rain could certainly dampen months and months of preparation. Marvin J. Ashton, then a member of the YMMIA general board, said, "Bertha was never bewildered or overpowered or defeated. . . . Some of us used to fret when it would threaten rain for our dance festivals. She didn't; she knew it would come out all right."[22]

One year when it began raining the day before the dance festival, the chairman of the dance committee phoned Bertha and asked if the presidency and general board would join with the committee members in a fast. Bertha recalled, "It just poured down, and in the morning we called the fire department and they pumped the water off of the stadium. They dried it out, and we put on our festival that night. President George Albert Smith came up to the fieldhouse; we always had prayer together in the fieldhouse before the program. It was an inspiration to see all those boys and girls kneeling in prayer before they went on the dance floor."[23]

Music festivals were also popular activities for June Conference, and similar festivals were encouraged for local production. In 1961, ward and stake MIAs were asked to produce the musical *Promised Valley* by Crawford Gates and Arnold Sundgaard, which had originally been produced in 1947 for the centennial of the pioneers' arrival in the Salt Lake Valley.

For four years, beginning in August 1954, the MIA general boards held a conference similar to June Conference in southern California so that the MIA leaders there would not have to travel to Utah. President David O. McKay addressed the first of these conferences at the famed Hollywood Bowl.

To counteract society's deteriorating moral climate during the 1950s, the YWMIA and YMMIA published and distributed a series of posters with the theme "Be Honest with Yourself." Such messages as "Great Men Pray," "Virtue Is Its Own Reward," "Fresh Up with Sunday," and "Living Prophets" were depicted. Popular and effective in reaching youth, the posters hung in meetinghouses throughout the Church. They were also reprinted in wallet-sized cards for each of the young men and women.

The duties of the YWMIA general board included supervising the Beehive House, which served until 1959 as a dormitory for eighty-five young women who came to Salt Lake City to work or attend school. The residents nicknamed it the "Behave House." Several times Bertha was called to go to the Beehive

House in the middle of the night when a girl had stayed out too late. She later said that her role was "to supervise the girls, see that they went to Church and keep them on the straight and narrow."[24] In addition, the YWMIA was responsible for the operation of the Lion House, which had a cafeteria in the basement for Church employees and meeting rooms on the upper floors for various study groups and classes.

For the most part, the YWMIA was financially self-sustaining, operating on receipts from the sale of manuals, pins, and awards; dues paid by ward members; and twenty-five cents from each *Improvement Era* subscription. The YWMIA was housed in the former Bishop's Building at 40 North Main Street. When the Relief Society moved into its own building in 1956, the YWMIA expanded its offices in the Bishop's Building.

During her tenure as YWMIA general president, Bertha worked with four YMMIA general superintendents: George Q. Morris, Elbert R. Curtis, Joseph T. Bentley, and G. Carlos Smith. One of their joint duties was serving as associate editors of the *Improvement Era.* In 1960 the editors inaugurated a section in the magazine for young people, titled "Era of Youth." The editors were Elder Marion D. Hanks and Elaine A. Cannon.

The general officers and boards of the two organizations worked closely together. The boards met each Wednesday evening for a general session, followed by separate committee meetings. Many of the activities committees were comprised of both YW and YM board members, while the age-group committees met separately. One member, W. Jay Eldredge, described the association of the young women's and the young men's boards as "working in concert."[25]

One of Bertha's most significant endeavors as YWMIA president was to encourage stake and ward leaders to train their youth for leadership. She frequently suggested, "Use your young people." "I don't feel sorry for tired leaders," she would add, reminding YWMIA workers that they needed to involve the young women in planning and carrying out activities and programs and not do it all themselves.[26]

An Able Administrator

Bertha Reeder was generous in giving credit for success to others. "I can't say enough for the counselors who worked with me and the general board," she remarked. "We worked together thirteen and a half years and we never had a cross word. Never [did] any of the workers ever [feel] like they were criticized; we never felt we had to get after anybody. They all seemed to want to do everything they could do and we just loved each other.

"A president never works alone, and she's only as good as her counselors and the workers she's with. The general president isn't good unless she gets the support of the wards and stakes. We felt we had the support of the wards and stakes because they were allowed to work on their own and a lot of them would come and ask to initiate a program."[27]

Those who worked with Bertha responded to the love, the warmth, and the confidence she placed in them. LaRue C. Longden, who served as Bertha's counselor during her entire administration, said, "She loved us and she knew our potential, but we didn't until she called us to work with her. . . . She had the ability to know that God gave us talents but some of us might not have developed them if it were not for her."[28]

"Bertha was a beautiful woman," said Marvin J. Ashton. "She had an instant personality; she could go into any stake, convention, or conference any place in the world and in an instant shake hands with people and they were her friends. She had a warm, friendly personality which rang true from the first moment you met her. She had a beautiful sense of humor; she loved to laugh; she loved to smile."[29]

Both Helena Larson Allen, Bertha's executive secretary, and Ruth Hardy Funk, a member of Bertha's general board who later served as seventh general president, remembered traveling to visit stakes with Bertha and making numerous stops along the way to see historical sites and the beauties of nature. Although Bertha was an adventurous outdoorswoman and traveler by car, she disliked flying and did not want to fly anywhere without a family member or friend to go with her. Yet she traveled widely as YWMIA president, visiting Europe, New Zealand, Australia, Mexico, Canada, Alaska, and Hawaii. She supported the National Council of Women and served as a delegate to council meetings held in Washington, D.C. She was also a member of the Travelers'

Aid Society and three literary clubs — the Acacia Club, the Classics Club, and the Children's Hour Club.

Fishing with Judge and her family provided Bertha with needed respite from her responsibilities, particularly after June Conference. She often remarked during the busy conference time, "I know that when this June Conference is over, there will be a trip to a stream where there will be a trout waiting with my name on it."[30]

Bertha and Judge enjoyed traveling together, and when diabetes hindered his mobility, she arranged for a wheelchair for him so that he could still travel. He died in March 1961, and Bertha was released from her service as general YWMIA president a few months later, on September 30. She had served in this calling for thirteen and one-half years.

Bertha Reeder's Last Years

On February 14, 1964, Bertha was married to I. L. (Lee) Richards, a man she had known for many years. After a ninety-day world honeymoon tour, they made their home in Ogden. "Lee has been so good to me," she wrote in her diary. "I respect and love him so much."[31]

When she was eighty-eight years old, Bertha fell and suffered a massive hematoma on her brain. After Lee's death in June 1981, she resided in a rest home in Pocatello, Idaho, near her daughter, Oertel. She died December 26, 1982, at the age of ninety. Her funeral was held in Ogden.

Bertha Stone Reeder's optimistic personality radiated her love of life, her love of people, and her love of the gospel of Jesus Christ. An adventurous woman, she loved to see the beauties of the world and found joy in the outdoors. Her graciousness and smile endeared her to everyone she met. Her love and confidence helped many people to see greater potential in themselves. Her creed was "the Lord comes first,"[32] and she followed that creed in every aspect of her long life.

6

Florence Smith Jacobsen
1961–1972

*L*ate one night in August 1965, Florence Jacobsen looked around the Joseph Smith Sr. home in Palmyra, New York, with others who had helped her refurbish it. Every detail was perfect. The windows, enlarged by later residents of the house, had been restored to their smaller size. Each original shrunken random-width board in the wooden floor had been moved over to fill in the cracks. New tongue-in-groove boards had been fashioned and used to fill in the space left from sliding over the original boards. Shingles similar to the ones used in the early 1830s had even replaced the modern shingles on the roof. From the rocking chair in the parlor to the handmade candles in each room, everything was consistent with the time period when the Smiths lived there.

"Let's light all the candles and walk through the home," Florence suggested. The warm glow of flickering light filled each room as she and the others lit the candles and turned off the electric lights. "It was like going back in time," she remembers. "We climbed the stairs, and I wondered how many times my great-grandfather Hyrum Smith, who helped build the house, had gone up and down those stairs. We walked slowly from room to room and imagined the Smiths living there—eating and sleeping and going through all the joy and the trauma surrounding that significant time in their lives. We sat in the parlor and envisioned the excitement that must have filled that room when young Joseph sent his sister Sophronia over to the original log cabin, where Hyrum and his wife Jerusha then lived, to get a box in which to place the plates he had received from the angel Moroni at the Hill Cumorah."

For Florence Jacobsen, who knows that care to meticulous detail can help recreate a setting that can take us back in time so we can experience history, such is the reward of refurbishing or restoring a home.

A Rich Heritage

Florence Smith Jacobsen is the granddaughter of two presidents of the Church, Heber J. Grant and Joseph F. Smith. She grew up in Salt Lake City on Eighth Avenue between A and B streets, surrounded by extended family. Her parents, Willard Richards and Florence Grant Smith, were the parents of six sons and two daughters: Willard Grant, Florence, Richards Grant, Briant Grant, Heber Joseph, Howard Grant, Sarah Ellen, and Paul Grant. Florence quickly became known as "Sis" to avoid confusion with her mother. Aunt Lutie—Lucy Grant Cannon, Florence's aunt and the fourth general president of the YWMIA— lived next door. President Grant lived on the other side of the Smiths. Several of Florence's aunts, uncles, and cousins lived in homes scattered throughout the surrounding blocks.

During Florence's childhood and her early married life, one of her two grandfathers served as president of the Church— first, Joseph F. Smith, and then, after President Smith's death, Heber J. Grant.

"I remember as a young child visiting Grandfather Smith in his home in the Beehive House," she says. "He used to lift me up on his knee and open a desk drawer and give me some candy mints or candy-coated almonds to eat. He was the kindest man I have ever known as his eyes radiated kindness."[1]

When Heber J. Grant became president of the Church, he chose to remain in his home rather than move to the Beehive House, which had previously been the president's official residence. As a result, Florence spent much of her childhood with him. She clearly remembers him "picking out the melody of Church hymns on the piano and loudly singing the songs."[2]

Life in the Smith household was busy and happy for Florence, the eldest daughter. Her father, a gentle man, had been protective and supportive of his own mother, and after he married, he treated his wife with the same solicitude. "There were eight of us children, and father had us so organized that the job never got too big for my mother," she said in a magazine interview. "He'd have us up at six o'clock calling, 'It's a beautiful morning! Time to get up.' And we all knew what we were supposed to do. . . . I never saw my mother scrub a floor. My father or my brothers always did it."[3]

From the time Florence was two until she was fifteen, her father served in the bishopric. He was also an officer at Zions Saving Bank and Trust Company. But though he was busy, he spent Saturdays with his children, usually taking them on tours of sites in and around the Salt Lake Valley. Sometimes they walked and sometimes they rode in a Stearns-Knight open touring car. "Father always told us the history of the places we visited," she remembers. "Then he'd bring us home and take all the boys and neighborhood kids to the Deseret Gym. Mother and I usually baked cookies or made candy. Then Father would buy Morrison meat pies and a quart of gravy on his way home and we'd have that for dinner. Those were happy memories."

Birthdays and Christmas were big family events, usually celebrated with dinner parties in the basement of Lucy Grant Cannon's home. The family would eat at a long table made of wooden planks on trestles. For Christmas, there were homemade gifts for everyone, and a Christmas tree decorated with taffy-filled cornucopias for visiting children.

A summer home in Emigration Canyon east of Salt Lake City served as a retreat for the extended Grant and Smith families. Florence and her cousins dug a stage out of the side of the mountain and performed their own plays. Sometimes they used Aunt Lucy's cabin in nearby Big Cottonwood Canyon.

Florence remembers tender moments as her parents shared stories from the lives of their ancestors. Her interest in Church history grew as she learned of these ancestors, most of whom had been leaders in the Church since its restoration in 1830. One of her favorites is her great-grandmother, Mary Fielding Smith, widow of Hyrum Smith. "The lives of my ancestors influenced me as much as anything else," she says. "I always wanted to be a stalwart like Mary Fielding, who was a little English lady, but very proper and, extremely courageous."

Having her grandfathers serve as president of the Church brought Church history and its buildings and artifacts into Florence's everyday life. She still remembers her feelings when she visited the Beehive House, where her Grandfather Smith lived, and her realization that Brigham Young had built this home and made many of its furnishings. Similar feelings filled her when she visited the home of Mary Fielding Smith.

"I have always been interested in things of historical significance," she once said in a newspaper interview. "Even when I was a little girl, if I saw a chair that belonged to a person from the past, I revered it, and I felt it was a privilege to see it. . . . For example, a flour barrel in one corner of the Lion House is a family heirloom. It came across the plains tied onto the Longstroth family wagon [Florence's second great-grandparents]. . . . I feel a part of these people and feel like it's a great privilege to be involved in these things to help preserve the past and pass it on to future generations."[4]

College, Career, and Courtship

Florence attended LDS High School on the same block as the Church Administration Building in downtown Salt Lake City. When she was fifteen, she took sewing lessons at the Lion House, which was then used by students of the high school for some classes. Possessing a natural gift for sewing and an eye for good design, she learned to make hats on a hat block, to crochet beaded bags, and to make lace.

After graduating from high school in 1930, Florence attended the University of Utah, where she developed her talents in fashion design, interior design, and architectural design as a home economics major. "I took historical architecture," she says. "My thesis was on historical fashions, and it was totally illustrated in color. I have been terrifically interested in it all my life."

When Florence signed up for a geology class at the university and went on a field trip, she found more than knowledge about geology—she met her future husband, Theodore C. Jacobsen. The class visited a large sandbar that had built up when the Great Salt Lake was much higher than it is today. Ted noticed Florence, who was climbing the sandy bar with her best friend and cousin, Edna Boyle.

"I wanted to be introduced to Florence," remembers Ted. "I knew Edna, so I climbed up behind them and pulled at their feet just a little bit so it was hard for them to get to the top. Finally Edna introduced me. I invited Florence to a fraternity party that night, but we didn't have a very good time. I thought I should ask her out one more time to make up for the first date, and that was when I became interested in her."[5]

Five years older than Florence, Ted Jacobsen was born in San Francisco. His father, Soren N. Jacobsen, had come alone as a boy of nineteen from Denmark to America to find work as a millwright (combination carpenter and mechanic). Once in America, he kept moving westward, eventually finding his way to Salt Lake City, where he met Anna M. Jensen, a convert to the Church from Norway. They married and moved to San Francisco, where he used his carpentry skills to help rebuild the city after the earthquake and fire of 1906. He also joined the Church, and the family moved back to Salt Lake City.[6]

Ted served a mission in Denmark. When he returned, he began studying engineering at the University of Utah and was active in a fraternity. Since Florence was vice president of her sorority, they were part of a close group of students who dated and attended parties together.

During the summers, Florence worked at the Utah Home Fire Insurance Company, typing and answering the telephone. After graduation in 1934, she got a job at the Salt Lake Knit company, where she soon became a pattern maker, a job requiring exacting skills. (Even now, she can still cut out a dress freehand.) She excelled in the work and was soon designing dresses.

Florence was fortunate to have been able to attend college and then get a good job during those early years of the Great Depression. She remembers the day when the effects of the Depression hit the Smith home. On that day Willard Smith gathered his family around the kitchen table and told them he and the other bank officers had made a difficult decision that afternoon. They could either retain full salaries and let half of the employees go or cut their own salaries and retain all the employees. They voted to cut their own salaries and preserve the jobs for others.

"It was tough," says Florence. "There were eight children, and two of my brothers were on missions and I was in college. My father said we were all going to have to pitch in and get jobs as well as cut back. I can remember making my clothes over and even taking mother's old clothes and redoing them. In fact, I once won first prize for taking an old velvet dress of mother's and making it into a formal for me."

The Smiths helped their hired girl find another job, and then the children divided up the housework. Florence's jobs included putting up all the lunches, cleaning the upstairs bathroom and her own bedroom, and dusting the living room, dining room, and alcove. On Saturdays, she ironed shirts for her father and brothers.

As difficult as things were for the Smiths, they were better off financially than many families. Florence remembers finding copies of hundreds of letters among her father's things after he died indicating that he had often personally loaned money to people when the bank couldn't give them a loan because they had no collateral—five hundred dollars to one, a thousand to another. This illustration of her father's generosity has served as a powerful example for Florence throughout her life.

Florence and Ted courted for more than two years. Ted remembers one of their dates that had a surprise ending: "My friend and I took our dates tobogganing once. As I took Florence down those steep hills from the 'U' on the hill near the University of Utah, we built up terrific speed. My friend and his date were right behind us. The snowbanks were very high on the streets and we couldn't stop when we came to the road so we took a ten-foot drop. Both of our dates ended up unconscious and slightly injured."[7]

During the depression, Ted quit school and went to work with his father, a contractor, whenever a job was available. While working on a building at Utah State Agricultural College in Logan, he finished his final year of engineering and graduated—nine interruption-filled years after he had started his college studies at the University of Utah. During these separations, he and Florence continued their courtship by correspondence.

Marriage and Family Life

Ted and Florence were married by President Heber J. Grant in the Salt Lake Temple on September 23, 1935. Their wedding breakfast was held at the Lion House, which had been recently redecorated by Florence's Aunt Lucy. The newly married couple lived for several months in Evanston, Wyoming, while Ted completed a contracting job building a new high school. Meanwhile, they bought a home in Salt Lake City on Harvard Avenue, through the block from Ted's parents. His father remodeled the home for them while they were in Evanston.

Florence and Ted's first child, Stephen Smith Jacobsen, was born May 28, 1938. Constant dehydration from the summer heat threatened his life, so Florence, her mother, and Stephen spent most of the hot summer in the Smiths' cabin in the higher elevation of Emigration Canyon, which was twenty degrees cooler than the Salt Lake Valley. Three years later, on October 1, 1941, Alan Smith Jacobsen was born; and four years after that, on November 20, 1945, Heber Smith Jacobsen joined the family.

As a contractor, Ted usually had to work half a day on Saturday. This was a difficult adjustment for Florence, who had such fond memories of her Saturday-morning adventures with her own father. But as the boys got a little older, Ted could see how important family outings were to them, and one Saturday he took his family fishing on the Snake River in Idaho. Florence and the three boys fished from the shore while Ted, in chest-high waders, walked into the river. Suddenly he stepped into deep water and disappeared right before Florence's eyes. "It was the most horrifying experience of my life," she remembers. "I thought 'He's gone! I'm a widow!' But miraculously, Ted was able to take off the waders and surface again. I said to him, 'Honey, I don't care if you ever take off Saturday again.'"

Despite this fearful moment, the Jacobsens continued to enjoy fishing together, and in 1961 they bought a cabin on Hebgen Lake in Montana near Yellowstone National Park. An excellent fisherman and cook, Florence, who isn't afraid of hard work, would clean the pans in which they cooked fish over an open fire by scrubbing them with sand until her hands were red.

The family enjoyed a few weeks at the ocean every summer at the family home on Balboa Island off the coast of California. The children loved fishing, swimming, water skiing, and lying in the sun. As they got older, they worked summers with Ted in his construction business. During these years, Ted served as bishopric counselor and then bishop of the Bonneville Ward. Florence became active in church, school, and community organizations, such as PTA, Red Cross, Cancer Society, and the University of Utah, and had a keen interest in politics.

Woven through Florence's executive skills is her love of and skill in homemaking. As a young mother, she often made costumes for various activities. She also excelled at knitting and needlepoint and in interior decorating. Christmas, always a special time during her childhood, retained its "larger than life" status in the Jacobsen home. Even today, handmade gifts, the preferred presents, make Christmas a year-round project, as she crochets afghans, stitches needlepoint pin cushions, or sews counted cross-stitch pictures and stores them in the family's "Christmas closet." Tradition surrounds the menus for the Christmas Eve dinner with relatives, the Christmas morning breakfast with the family, and a large dinner on December 26 for extended family. Her Aunt Lucy taught her how to make fondant and dip chocolates, and delicious homemade candies have long been an important part of her entertaining. "I love to be at a social gathering with Florence, and hear her happy laughter across the room," said Ted. "That has been one of my secret feelings about her. She has such a lovely laugh, and it gives me a good feeling to hear it."[8]

Another of Florence's gifts is an ability to keep track of details and to organize people and events. A needlepoint cover encases her address book, which is filled with names, addresses, and phone numbers of hundreds of friends and acquaintances and a list of the clubs and groups to which she belongs. She keeps records of the names of everyone to whom she gives or from whom she receives a Christmas present or card. Family photographs, awards, and newspaper clippings fill neat scrapbooks. While serving as general president of YWMIA, she listed the name of every person who helped with June Conference, and to each she sent a handwritten thank-you note. She also keeps an updated list of every talk she gives and where she gives it.

Missionary Service and an Unexpected Call

In 1955, when the Jacobsen boys were teenagers, Ted was called to serve as president of the Eastern States Mission, and the family moved to New York City. They lived in the mission home at 973 Fifth Avenue, across the street from the Metropolitan Museum of Art and Central Park. Her years in the mission field proved to be an influential period in the development of Florence's leadership skills. She served as mission Relief Society president and vice chairman of the mission auxiliary board, and helped to write manuals and publish a monthly bulletin for each auxiliary. She also gained an understanding of the many challenges that Church members face in the mission field.

Soon after her return from New York in 1959, Florence was called to serve on the YWMIA general board. President Bertha S. Reeder assigned her to the Gleaner committee. Calling upon her experience in the mission field, Florence served as co-chairman of a committee to write a manual of activities and lessons for use by families who were isolated from other members. Then the concept was expanded, and a manual was prepared for a small MIA comprised of two or three families who lived in closer proximity. "I think those books were some of the best ever produced in the Church," she said. "They helped isolated families feel included as part of the larger Church program."

Years of Challenges and Rewards

Always an excellent hostess and cook, Florence rarely experienced a failure when hosting a dinner party. One notable exception was the day she was called to serve as general president of the YWMIA. Two of her sons, Stephen and Alan, had been activated with the Utah National Guard in the Berlin Crisis of 1961, and she had planned a going-away dinner for them on a Friday evening in late September. That afternoon President David O. McKay called her to his office and asked her to serve as general president of the YWMIA. She accepted, but she was stunned at the call and unable to think of anything else when she returned home to finish preparing dinner. Her sons realized that something was unusual when the food didn't taste quite right, but she could not tell them of her new calling yet.

At general conference on October 1, 1961, Bertha Reeder and her counselors, Emily Bennett and LaRue Longden, were released as the YWMIA presidency. Florence S. Jacobsen was sustained as the general president of the YWMIA, with Margaret Romney Jackson and Dorothy Porter Holt as her counselors. As the presidency set out to lead 300,000 young women, they sometimes ended up in Bertha's living room, asking for help and counsel. "Bertha would answer our questions," says Florence, "then she'd laugh and say, 'There's nothing to it. You'll be fine. Say your prayers and you'll be blessed.' "

"It is my prayer that we can be so dedicated that not one single girl in this great Church will be forgotten," Florence declared at the area conference at Manchester, England, August 28, 1971.[9] This concern for the individual was of primary importance for her and her counselors and and their large general board, which fluctuated between fifty-eight and seventy members. Their years of service were filled with preparations for dance and music festivals, roadshows, parent and youth programs, new manuals, leadership training, youth conferences, and many other responsibilities, but underlying it all was a concern for the individual. Young women learned to keep personal record books, worked toward yearly Individual Awards as part of the girls' program, and served in class presidencies.

Though Florence was usually caught up in far-reaching YWMIA programs and restoration projects, she took time to meet and encourage "the one," often on a private and individual basis. When the presidency visited Japan for an area conference, they met Miyuki Uchida, a seventeen-year-old Laurel whose face had been severely burned in an accident when she was a baby. They made arrangements for her to come to America for plastic surgery. Laurels in many areas held service projects known as "Miyuki Days" to raise money for her transportation and surgery.

The only Latter-day Saint in her family, Miyuki came to Salt Lake City and lived with Margaret Jackson for eight months while a local plastic surgeon reconstructed her face.[10]

During these years of miniskirts and other signs of youth rebellion, dress standards took on a high priority in the MIA. In talks, seminars, and youth conferences, leaders reinforced the principle of modesty in dress and actions. Counselor Dorothy Holt remembers a testimony meeting at a youth conference where a young lady said that she had planned on wearing miniskirts as soon as she left home for college in the fall, but now, after hearing the counsel of the YWMIA, she had decided to maintain more modest dress standards.[11]

Florence had seen how the Church's programs for young men, such as annual Explorer conferences, had taught her sons responsibility and independence, and she wanted the same kinds of experiences for the young women. As a result, a general Laurel conference was held in 1970 on the Brigham Young University campus. It was planned as a teaching conference to help the young women learn leadership skills. A steering committee of five Laurels was called to head the conference, with other committees of Laurels selected for various activities and programs. Florence and members of the general board worked with these committees, encouraging them to pray as they worked through their plans step by step and to consider how the young women would react to each part of their program.

Each stake and mission in the United States and Canada was invited to send five second-year Laurels and one leader to the week-long conference. The three thousand young women who attended were then asked to plan and conduct similar conferences in their own areas. "I still have mothers and young women call and say, 'That Laurel conference changed my life,'" Florence says. "President Harold B. Lee was one of the speakers, and he said that the conference was 'inspired and one of the finest things that's ever happened in our church.'"

Under Florence's direction, the YWMIA camp and other activity programs continued to grow. Each year, activities surrounding June Conference became the crown jewels of the YWMIA year. Excitement filled the air as thousands of youth leaders attended parent-youth programs, theme presentations,

Improvement Era and M Men and Gleaner banquets, camp programs, arts festivals, and general and department sessions.

In addition to the programs for the Beehive, Mia Maid, Laurel, and Gleaner classes, the YWMIA was responsible with the YMMIA for the Young Marrieds program and for activities and classwork for Special Interests (single adults over twenty-five). The general superintendent of YMMIA served as general manager of the *Improvement Era,* and Florence was the associate general manager. A joint general board committee oversaw magazine subscription drives in wards, stakes, and missions. The executives and members of the two boards also helped to organize the Mormon Youth Symphony and to establish an outdoor theater on the site of the future Church Office Building, across Main Street from Temple Square, where performances of *Promised Valley* were presented on summer evenings. Later the Lyric Theater in downtown Salt Lake City was renovated and renamed Promised Valley Playhouse, and the musical moved to an indoor theater that also was used for other Church-sponsored productions.

Restoring the Past

When Florence became YWMIA president, she had no idea that the YWMIA was responsible for the operation of the Lion House until she saw her budget. Noting that only the cafeteria was in the black, she suggested that the home be restored for use as a social center. But soon she learned that there were plans to tear it down. With all the tenacity of her great-grandmother Mary Fielding Smith, she said that she'd "be out there sitting in front of the bulldozer" if it were torn down. Apparently, many others felt the same way because eventually the thinking changed on the subject. It was decided that the Lion House would be restored, under the direction of Florence Jacobsen.

The home was closed for five years for major reconstruction and renovation. Florence insisted that every detail of the furnishings be absolutely authentic. The original carpets in the home in the 1800s had been woven with seventeen colors. When she learned that modern-day looms could weave only twelve colors, she negotiated with the carpet manufacturer to hire five extra weavers to hand-lay the additional colors.

Finally the restoration was completed and the home was nearly ready to reopen. "I can remember when Florence invited all the board members down to the Lion House to help clean it," says Helena Allen, YWMIA secretary during Florence's administration. "All of us, including Florence, washed windows and cleaned every corner of that entire building."[12] At the grand reopening in 1968, board members, wearing pioneer dresses, helped direct guests from room to room and downstairs to the cafeteria, now renamed the Lion House Pantry.

In the middle of the Lion House renovation project, Florence was asked in April 1966 to redecorate the Joseph Smith Sr. home near Palmyra, New York, in time for the Hill Cumorah Pageant in August. She was thrilled. The Hill Cumorah area was part of the Eastern States Mission, and when she had visited the home while living in New York, she had recognized that work needed to be done on it. Now she welcomed the opportunity to help make it authentic to the early 1800s, when the Smiths had lived there. Completing the project under a tight deadline while also planning and carrying out June Conference presented enormous challenges, but Florence, with the help of Margaret Jackson and others, pitched in and completed the assignment in time for the pageant.

When the YWMIA observed its centennial worldwide in 1969, a major focal point for the celebration was the Lion House, where Brigham Young had rung a prayer bell to call his daughters together to form the Retrenchment Association in 1869. In honor of the centennial, Florence placed a prayer bell in a niche in the front hall of the newly restored home, and a YWMIA history, featuring collages of historical photographs, was published. At June Conference, young women dressed in costumes of many nationalities participated in special all-girl productions at the dance festival; and drama presentations, camp programs, sports events, banquets, testimony meetings, receptions, and other activities centered around the centennial theme.

During her years as YWMIA president, Florence served as a member of the Church Arts and Sites committee under the direction of Elder Mark E. Petersen of the Council of the Twelve.

Committee members reviewed letters from persons who wished to donate artifacts, furniture, even homes to the Church. Elder Petersen would read each letter and then ask if the committee members thought they should accept the donation.

"I always answered yes," Florence recalls. "Someone would ask, 'Where are we going to store it?' and I'd say, 'In the basement of the Bureau of Information on Temple Square.' Since Ted was the director of Temple Square during those years, I had ready access to the bureau basement."

Florence enjoyed using her talents to improve anyplace where she lived or worked, including the mission home in New York City and the YWMIA offices. Before she was released as president of the YWMIA in 1972, she had been involved with the restoration or refurbishing of the Wilford Woodruff and Brigham Young homes in Nauvoo, Illinois, and the Peter Whitmer home in Fayette, New York, in addition to the Lion House and the Joseph Smith Sr. home.

A Close Friendship

As president of the YWMIA, Florence was a member of the National Council of Women (NCW) and of the International Council of Women (ICW). And as general president of the Relief Society, Belle S. Spafford was also a member of the two councils. They both enjoyed serving on committees and participating in meetings of the groups. Florence served on the ICW Child and Family committee from 1965 to 1973, and in 1966 she and Sister Spafford were official delegates from the NCW to the eighteenth triennial conference of the ICW in Tehran, Iran. In 1970 they attended the annual convention of ICW in Bangkok, taking with them a display of 120 items of Native Americans art. From 1974 to 1976 Sister Spafford served as president and Florence as third vice president of the NCW. After their terms were over, they were asked to rewrite the NCW constitution and bylaws.

The two auxiliary presidents traveled together often in connection with their church responsibilities. In 1962, they visited the ten stakes in England, Scotland, Holland, Germany, and Switzerland and held Relief Society and YWMIA conventions.

"We all felt that the greatest frontier in the Church for MIA is in the mission field," Florence said.[13]

Later, in honor of Sister Spafford, Florence helped establish the Belle S. Spafford Endowed Chair in the Graduate School of Social Work at the University of Utah.

A New Career

At a special meeting in the Church Administration Building on November 9, 1972, the YWMIA general presidency and board were released. For six months after her release, Florence busied herself with furnishing a condominium in Palm Springs, California, that she and Ted had recently purchased. Her mother went to California with her (her father had died earlier), and the two women enjoyed the warm sunshine and trips to Los Angeles to visit Florence's sister, Sarah.

During this time Florence had no idea that another career loomed on the horizon, an opportunity as demanding as YWMIA president. Then one day in April 1973, she received a call from President Harold B. Lee, who asked if she would be willing to return to Salt Lake City and become Church curator. She accepted. Plunging into her new position, she set out to inventory and catalog the Church's art, historical possessions, and buildings; arrange for copyrights and security for these valuable works; and work out ways to handle additional donations. She gathered a corps of volunteers to help her, and soon she was able to hire curators who specialized in such areas as architecture, historical art, and art conservation. Eventually, she supervised thirty-eight employees, and her title was changed to director of Historic Arts and Sites.

Over the years, Florence directed the organization of the jumbled collections in underground storerooms on Temple Square and made sure that artwork and other irreplaceable artifacts were cleaned, cataloged, and stored in climate-controlled areas. One need soon became apparent: a museum in which to display some of the artifacts and art so that members and nonmembers could enjoy them. Her dream was fulfilled with construction of the Museum of Church History and Art on West Temple, across the street from the west gate of Temple

Square. Her goals also included museum accreditation, uniform computer systems among museums and major historians in the state, and an effective loan policy. As a result, some treasures owned by the Church have been placed on permanent loan to museums throughout the world.

In 1976, when the U.S. Bicentennial was observed, Florence oversaw the development of an exhibit on the early Mormon pioneers for the Smithsonian Institution in Washington, D.C. The pioneers were of interest to the Smithsonian because as a people with their own government, society, educational system, currency, and military, they represented well the theme of the Bicentennial display, "We the People." As with other projects she conceived and directed, Florence achieved a high level of excellence with this exhibit.

"This is a lady whose life has made a difference," says Richard Oman, a curator at the museum in Salt Lake City, "and it has had a major impact on the Church. Her gift was creating institutions. With a very fast learning curve and an ability to adjust rapidly to new situations, Florence could make decisions easily and quickly. By surrounding herself with educated, capable people, she had access to the best advice possible. This was a lady capable of growth and change. She was a tigress for a good idea—a very eloquent tigress."[14]

Florence continued to supervise the restoration of many Church buildings, including the Promised Valley Playhouse and Brigham Young Forest Farmhouse in Salt Lake City; the E. B. Grandin building in Palmyra, New York; the Brigham Young home in St. George, Utah, and the Jacob Hamblin home in nearby Santa Clara; the Pine Valley Chapel north of St. George; the Newell K. Whitney store in Kirtland, Ohio; and the interior of the Manti Temple.

Through the years Florence has received numerous awards and honors. In October 1968 she received the National Council of Women "Woman of Conscience" award for her service to youth and her "efforts to promote respect for the rights and freedoms of others."[15] Students at Ricks College in Rexburg, Idaho, selected her to receive their Exemplary Womanhood Award in 1974, and BYU women students gave her a similar award in 1980. Others have included a special award of recognition from the Church at a Master M Man and Golden Gleaner program in 1973, a silver plate in appreciation for her devotion to the youth of the Church;[16] and the 1989 Utah Museum Association Award of Merit.

Instilling the Past in the Future

Florence Jacobsen's strong feelings toward heritage and family have ensured her willingness to invest time and energy into the well-being of her grandchildren and nieces and nephews. She is concerned about those who face serious challenges and looks for ways to help them. She refuses to lose hope in their future.[17]

"You can really tie the living of the gospel in the tradition of the family," she said in a newspaper interview. "I've started the young women on needlepoint pieces, trying to teach them the art young pioneer girls were required to learn when they did samplers. On their eighth birthday, I have given each of the girls a piece of antique jewelry that I got from one of my grandmothers. I have written letters telling how I received these pieces and how much I treasured them. I instructed the girls that whenever they are tempted to do anything wrong, the jewelry should remind them they were not to come to any kind of wrong-doing."[18]

"Florence is like her father, a perfectionist with unlimited energy," Ted observes. "She has made good use of the years of her life."[19] Few have accomplished as much with their lives as has she. A devoted wife, mother, and homemaker, she has served extensively in the Church, in the community, and in the National and International Councils of Women, and in preserving the past she dearly loves. Florence Jacobsen is an example of the good one person can do when she is committed to a cause and uses her talents to bring that cause to fruition.

7

Ruth Hardy Funk
1972–1978

At the closing session of the 1975 June Conference in the Salt Lake Tabernacle, when MIA leaders traditionally sang "Carry On," the conductor passed his baton to Ruth Hardy Funk, general president of the Young Women, to lead the song. He told the audience, "Because of her great love for youth and her dedication to them, we feel it only fitting that she conduct this song at this special time." She stepped to the conductor's stand and with fervor led the congregation in singing "O youth of the noble birthright, / Carry on, carry on, carry on."[1] That experience typified the focus of Ruth Funk's life—music and youth, along with love and devotion to her family.

Ancestry and Early Life

Ruth's maternal grandfather, George Reynolds, was born in 1842 in the Marylebone district of London. When he was nine years old, his grandmother's maid, a Mormon, began taking the boy to meetings of the Paddington Branch of the Church. Almost immediately he accepted the missionaries' teachings as true, and he pleaded with his parents to allow him to be baptized. They refused. Though he was discouraged, George continued to attend meetings in secret whenever he could. His parents, hoping that he would forget the Church, sent him to live with relatives in Paris when he was twelve. He returned to London about two years later and began attending a different branch of the Church. There, at age fourteen, he was baptized and confirmed—to the intense displeasure of his parents. At nineteen, George became a full-time missionary in London, and four years later, in 1865, he emigrated to Utah. A fine writer, he was secretary to five presidents of the Church, beginning with Brigham Young. Later in his life, he compiled the *Concordance to the Book of Mormon* and served as a member of the First Council of the Seventy.[2]

George Reynolds's third wife, Mary Goold, also an English convert, was Ruth's grandmother. Ruth, as the second oldest grandchild, was close to Mary and remembered that she was "always the Relief Society president." Mary instilled in Ruth her great reverence for life and beautiful things — especially roses — and a deep and abiding faith in the Savior.

Ruth's paternal grandparents, Thomas Henry and Mary Ann Jenkins Hardy, were from second-generation Latter-day Saint Welsh mining families who were hardworking but fun-loving. Music was, according to Ruth, "an important part of their lives." The night before her great-grandfather Jenkins died at age eighty-six, he won a waltz contest at Saltair, a resort west of Salt Lake City on the shores of the Great Salt Lake. Later, Ruth's grandfather Hardy became winter caretaker at Saltair, and she remembers spending Christmas afternoons roller-skating on the dance floor of the pavilion there.

Though the Hardys were not active in the Church, Mary Ann encouraged Fred, their oldest child, to go to church and take his four younger sisters. Ruth described him as having been "born with an impassioned testimony and devotion to the Lord." He became a dentist, a semiprofessional baseball player, and a fine musician.

Fred Hardy grew up in the Nineteenth Ward in Salt Lake City, as did Polly Reynolds, the daughter of George and Mary Goold Reynolds. Polly waited for Fred while he served a mission to England. When he returned, they married the day before he left for dental school at Northwestern University in Chicago. Since Polly, the second of nine children, helped support her mother and younger brothers and sisters by teaching school, she stayed home until the beginning of the next school year before joining him in Chicago. Ruth, Fred and Polly's first child, was born February 11, 1917, in Chicago. When Fred completed dental school, the family returned to Salt Lake City.

Ruth, who grew up in an environment where she was unconditionally loved and encouraged to develop her abilities, has described her childhood as "truly exceptional." The oldest of four children and the only girl, she inherited her passion for music from her father. Her earliest childhood recollection is of her mother telling her, "When you see your daddy coming, start winding up the phonograph." Ruth usually put on her father's favorite recording, of Caruso singing *Pagliacci.* He had a good tenor voice and would burst into singing whatever was playing when he entered the house. He never called his children to dinner or to go to church; rather, he signaled them by playing the piano.

Ruth began her piano studies at the age of six. Her father promised her that as soon as she could play Mendelssohn's "Rondo Capriccioso," he would buy her a grand piano. By the time she was twelve, Ruth earned her piano by playing not only the Mendolssohn piece at her first solo recital, but fifteen other pieces as well.

As Ruth grew up, she often arose at four o'clock to practice. Many times her mother pleaded with her to stop so she could get ready for school. As much as she loved practicing, Ruth was "bored stiff" with scales. But knowing they were essential to technical development, she devised a method of reading a book propped on the piano while playing scales and exercises. As a child, she especially loved the works of Chopin, Beethoven, and Mozart. Later she became enchanted with Debussy and the Impressionistic composers. After she started teaching piano herself, she was enraptured with Bach, Prokofiev, and Khatchaturian.

Polly and Fred enjoyed hearing Ruth play, and Ruth admitted to "always finding the right time to play," including after dinner when the dishes needed to be done or when other work was waiting. She also found that her piano playing got her out of taking a sewing class in high school. She put off taking sewing, something she did not like or do well, until her senior year. Then, because the sewing room was right next to the choir room, the choral teacher would borrow her every day to accompany the choir. At the end of the semester, Ruth had not even begun her required sewing project. The very strict sewing teacher never allowed students to work on their projects outside of class, but she made an exception in Ruth's case. She handed her the untouched fabric and told her to bring the project back completed—and she didn't care who did it. Ruth's mother, an excellent seamstress, did a beautiful job on the project, and when Ruth handed the completed item to her teacher and started to explain that her mother had done it, the teacher interrupted her and said, "I don't care. I don't even want to know who did it. I couldn't bear to have you in my class another semester. You will receive a D-minus."

Polly, a keenly intellectual woman, a scholar of the scriptures, and an artist, demanded excellence of herself and of her children. Ruth was not as fastidious as her mother and would rather get housework over with and go on to something more enticing. Once when she hurried through scrubbing the kitchen floor and only swiped the middle, her mother threw a bucket of water on the floor. By the time Ruth mopped the water out of all the corners, she knew what it meant to clean a floor thoroughly. Her fondest memories of her mother were the many hours they spent together as she drove Polly, who didn't drive, to the temple, to YLMIA general board meetings, to give book reviews of *Jesus the Christ*, shopping, and to other appointments. "My understanding and love of the gospel and for all of God's children were molded during these driving hours," she said.

Ruth's three brothers were all born at home. She was only two years old when Frederick was born, but she vividly remembers the events surrounding the births of Howard and Grant. She was the first one to hold the babies when her aunt Millie Martsen, the midwife, brought them from the bedroom where they were born.

Ruth enjoyed the influence of her aunt Alice Louise Reynolds, a professor of English at Brigham Young University, an editor of the *Relief Society Magazine*, and a member of the Relief Society general board. Although Alice lived in Provo, she often shared Ruth's room in the Hardy home whenever she was in Salt Lake. In Alice, Ruth found a stimulating companion who shared great literature with her, sent her postcards from her world travels, and introduced her to fascinating people.

Some Difficult Decisions

Because Ruth's musical prowess often put her into adult circles, she felt comfortable in the company of people older than she. When musicians and pianists visited Salt Lake City, she frequently performed for them in her own home, her teacher's studio, or various other settings. One renowned pianist, Leopold Godowsky, heard her play when she was in high school and suggested that she go to New York to continue her musical studies and train to become a concert pianist. Her father, greatly concerned about Ruth's future, consulted with Tracy Y. Cannon, chairman of the Church music committee and a close family friend. One Sunday the Hardy family and Brother Cannon fasted and prayed about the problem. Ruth, who was very close to her father, told him, "Daddy, no one but my Heavenly Father loves me more than you and Mother. No one else better knows how much I love music. I want you to make the decision." Her mother offered the prayer to end the fast. Then, while Polly and Ruth were preparing dinner in the kitchen, Fred and Brother Cannon consulted in the living room.

"I was beautifully and gently told by my father that our Heavenly Father had other things in mind for me than the pursuit of a career that could take on a dimension that could swallow up the more important opportunities I would be given," Ruth recalled. "He said I should remain in Salt Lake and continue my musical education but that I should not pursue a concert career. . . . The Lord knew I couldn't handle both that and the other major experiences that he wanted me to have. In no way can anything in music compare with motherhood and serving the Lord and knowing his scriptures and his doctrine. I feel I was guided by inspiration and I am grateful. Now the answer isn't going to be the same for everybody. Some women can and do manage it. I wouldn't ever suggest the fact that this was what the Lord wanted for anybody else but me. He knew my obsession."

Ruth decided to attend the University of Utah and to major in music education. She performed extensively as a soloist and as an accompanist and found time for involvement in other

activities, such as serving as a class officer, as president of her
sorority, and on various committees and councils.

Ruth fell in love with and became engaged to a friend from
high school, a fine violinist with whom she spent many hours
playing concertos and sonatas. They shared intellectual and cultural interests—but not religious beliefs. While Ruth was in
California accompanying the Male Glee Club on a concert tour,
she received word from her parents that she was to take the
next train home: her grandmother Hardy was dying and wanted
to see her. Her father met her at the depot and drove her directly
to see her grandmother, who had been in a coma for two days.
When Ruth entered the bedroom and spoke, her grandmother
opened her eyes and said, "Ruth, you can never be happy mar-
rying your young man. He will never hold the priesthood." Those
were her last words. Later, Ruth broke off her engagement.

Music played an important part in Ruth's meeting her future
husband. When she played a solo on the university's homecom-
ing assembly, Marcus Christopher Funk noticed her and asked
a friend who she was. He called her for a date, but they were
not able to get together for two months. Their first date was to
the senior class prom. That night, Ruth said, "by the time I was
at the foot of our street, I knew. I really knew. He just personified
everything that I had dreamed of." Marcus felt the same way.
"Both of us knew that something very special had happened,"
he recalled, "and we moved forward with our relationship quite
fast."[3]

Ruth accepted Marcus's ring a month later but didn't tell
her parents for another month, fearing they would think she
was in love on the rebound. She graduated from the University
of Utah in June 1938. Since she and Marcus planned to marry
in December and she would be accompanying Marcus in pursuit
of his degree in dental surgery, she sought a half-year teaching
position. The only one she could find was with a first-grade
class whose teacher had become ill. She taught seventy-five
children in two separate sessions each day.

At that time, the school district had a policy that allowed
each teacher to decide whether she would accept a physically
impaired child in her class. The parents of such a child brought
their son to Ruth's class. "I was young," she said. "I didn't know

a thing about handicapped children, but I remember looking at him and thinking, 'How can I turn him down? How can you say no?' I said, 'Of course I'll take him.' "

The boy had many physical problems, but Ruth's response to him was one of love. She said, "For reasons I really can't know, except the influence of the Spirit of the Lord and my continuous love of everything that breathes, which I think I inherited from my father, I loved him. I loved him right from the beginning." Because she loved him, the other first-graders responded positively and rejoiced in his accomplishments. "I learned the great lesson that one of the reasons God gives us the handicapped is to help to refine the souls of those of us who care for and teach and nurture children. We all have handicaps and must be our brother's keeper."

Marriage and Family

On December 31, 1938, Ruth and Marcus were married in the Salt Lake Temple, and they left by train that night for Washington, D.C., where he would take predental chemistry courses. Within a week after arriving in Washington, Ruth had a job as a substitute teacher. She left at eight in the morning and came home at six, walking several miles each way to save money. Marcus attended school from four in the afternoon to eleven at night, then worked from midnight until six in the morning at the Federal Reserve Bank. "Literally we did not see each other, except on Sundays," Ruth said. "Most of our early honeymooning was done by notes that we left here and there, which was a unique way to start a marriage, and I wouldn't recommend it to anyone." Marcus taught Sunday School in their Washington ward, and Ruth served on the stake Primary board.

Although the newlyweds had few pieces of furniture, they bought an old upright piano for twenty-five dollars. When they moved to Chicago the next fall so Marcus could attend dental school at Northwestern University in Chicago, the first item they purchased for their new apartment was a used piano.

Since teaching jobs at that time were scarce, with preference given to men and to single-parent mothers, Ruth applied for a job that required typing. She had never taken a typing course, but she believed that her years of practicing the piano would help prepare her to take the typing test. For two weeks she practiced typing as diligently as she had ever practiced the piano, and she got the job over eighty other applicants. She later became office manager for a staff of twenty-five.

Ruth was called as a counselor in the YWMIA presidency of the Chicago Stake, which at that time extended to Milwaukee, Wisconsin; Fort Wayne, Indiana; and Rockford, Illinois. Since her previous church callings had involved music and activities, this position gave her broader experience in Church administration.

Marcus was a senior in dental school when Pearl Harbor was attacked in December 1941 and the United States entered World War II. As a member of the Navy Reserve, he was able to complete his studies before reporting for active duty. He was assigned to the Marines, first in San Diego, California, and then at Camp Pendleton, near the town of Fallbrook. By then Ruth found out she was pregnant—something she had longed for during their four years of marriage. Because they could not obtain adequate housing, she returned home to Salt Lake City. Their first daughter, Nancy Ruth, was born July 11, 1943. Three months later, Marcus was able to get a weekend pass to come home to give her a name and a blessing.

Ruth and Nancy joined Marcus for six months before he was sent overseas on a cruiser, the *Louisville*. His ship was attacked twice by Japanese planes. During one of those attacks, a group of men with whom he had been conversing only seconds before were all killed. Unknowingly he had moved away just in time, and his life was spared.

While Marcus was on active duty, Ruth and Nancy returned to Salt Lake City, where Ruth was able to find an apartment in the tight housing market. At Marcus's instruction, she also bought a dental practice for him before he returned to Utah, since office space was nearly impossible to find. When the family was reunited, once more their first purchase was a piano for Ruth—this time a grand. Though Marcus had little interest in music, he wanted Ruth to be happy. She also needed a piano to teach lessons.

The Funks' second daughter, Allyson Marie, was born April

24, 1947. Five days later Lucy Grant Cannon, YWMIA general president, and her two counselors visited Ruth and called her to serve on the general board. Ruth's mother, Polly, had been on the general board for the past eighteen years, so mother and daughter would serve together.

Ruth was assigned to the music committee and to the Junior Girls committee, which developed the lesson manuals as well as the rose symbol for girls sixteen through eighteen years of age. She accompanied the June Conference music and dance festivals. When Lucy Grant Cannon was released in 1948, all the board members were released as well. The new YWMIA president, Bertha Stone Reeder, called Ruth to her board but requested that Polly assist Ruth by helping care for her children.

Ruth and Tabernacle organist Roy M. Darley, representing the YMMIA, comprised the music committee, which gave them numerous assignments to fill: writing or reviewing the yearly music supplement; providing music for June Conference; submitting music for the monthly *Leader* magazine, which was sent to stake MIA officers; and teaching basic music skills through lessons in the manual and in training sessions.

Bertha Reeder believed that everyone who wanted to participate in the June Conference music festival should be given that opportunity. Although the logistics and rehearsals were more complicated than for previous 400-participant festivals, three thousand singers filled the choir seats and balcony of the Tabernacle for June Conference in 1949. "It was glorious," according to Ruth. "The Lord really had a hand in it. We couldn't have done it ourselves. It was humanly impossible for what was done to have been done. It was totally in the Lord's hands, and Roy and I were able to be his instruments."

Family Support

Ruth and Marcus spent two years designing a home and were ready to break ground when the Korean War broke out in 1950. Since Marcus, the senior reserve dental officer in Utah, was subject to being called up, the Funks decided against building and bought their first and only home in Salt Lake City. George Hardy (Judd), their son, was born May 10, 1951, and six years later, on July 31, 1957, Jennie Jo was born. The four children all studied and excelled in music, each specializing on a different instrument or in voice: Nancy, cello; Allyson, violin; Judd, voice; and Jennie Jo, piano. Ruth continued teaching piano, and one of Jennie Jo's favorite memories as a child was "waking up on Saturday morning to the music of one of Mother's students, even though it was often at six o'clock in the morning."[4]

Because of the importance Ruth and Marcus placed on family activities, they were the last ones in the neighborhood to acquire a television set. But, in tune with their philosophy of activity, they were among the first to buy a boat. According to Jennie Jo, their trips to Lake Powell in southern Utah were "tops, the absolutely best family excursions."[5] The family also enjoyed outings in canyons and parks in the Salt Lake City area. Nancy remembered, "My mother never did anything in the ordinary way; she did everything with a flair. Our birthday parties were always wonderful, creative events that had a theme around which everything was planned."[6]

Nevertheless, Ruth's church and civic commitments frequently kept her away from home and her children. Her mother arrived every Wednesday at noon, the day of general board meeting, to take over for her. The only other person who cared for the Funk children besides their mother and grandmother was their nanny, Edla Olson, whom Ruth described as "a gift from God," though Ruth later admitted that "having me away so much was harder on my children than I realized."

When Nancy, the eldest daughter, was old enough, she was responsible for preparing dinner on general board meeting nights. She said, "I always had a great sense of pride at the contribution my mother was making. For a number of years I participated in the June Conference music festivals, playing my cello in the orchestra. I also enjoyed my associations with Mother's co-workers and friends."[7]

Marcus, supportive of Ruth and the extra efforts she always put into her assignments, told his children, "I am not a bit surprised at her callings. I knew when I married her that she wasn't an ordinary woman."[8] The Funks' daughter Allyson said, "I missed not having my mother home, but I never once heard my father murmur or complain about her assignments" —

whether they were meetings at Church headquarters or trips to the field throughout the world. "My father was extremely loyal to my mother," she continued. "He wasn't the bottlewasher or housekeeper support—because we had Mrs. Olson who took care of those things—but he supported Mom by encouraging her and never complaining."[9] "It was really no sacrifice," Marcus said. "I was serving through her. I always liked the old saying, 'He also serves who only stands and waits.' "[10]

A New Calling

As chairmen of the MIA music committee, Ruth and George I. Cannon, Lucy Grant Cannon's son, coproduced *Papa and the Playhouse*, a musical commemorating the one-hundredth anniversary of the Salt Lake Theater, for the 1962 June Conference. As with all her endeavors, Ruth worked with energy and enthusiasm on this production. She had more time than most people, for throughout her adult years she found she needed only about four to five hours of sleep a night. She said about her seemingly endless capacity to work, "Every morning I'd wake up with pure excitement about what the day might hold and with hopes that there would be surprises along the way. I guess that's why I've needed so little sleep, because I could hardly wait to wake up to see what was going to happen that day. I've always had the excitement for the dawn and the promises of life, even when it comes to some of the most horrendous challenges. I just love challenges." She also realized that not being a concert pianist or vocal performer suited her well, for she said, "I'm really the happiest when I am behind the scenes seeing people maximize their talents."

Following the 1962 conference, Elder Marion G. Romney called her on the telephone and changed her assignment from the MIA music committee to the Church correlation committee. Ruth's response was, "What in the world is correlation?" Elder Romney invited her to an orientation meeting at which Elder Harold B. Lee discussed the work of correlation. Ruth was assigned to the adult correlation committee, one of three committees formed to address the needs of children, youth, and adults. All curriculum and printed materials would be correlated

and evaluated through these committees so that there was con-
tinuity, completeness, and unity in gospel teaching. For the next
ten years, Ruth served first on the adult, then on the youth
correlation committee. She participated in the refocusing of
instructional design and development. With her organizational
skills, she developed a visible framework to chart lesson topics
and sequence in the curriculum.

While Ruth was serving in the demanding correlation assignment, she also found herself returning to schoolteaching.
She had not planned to return to teaching, but in 1966, with
her children in school, she agreed to teach junior high school
choral classes for a friend who was to have surgery. She ended
up teaching the entire year, and the next year she substituted
for another choral director.

In 1969, Lorraine Bowman, the choral director at East High
and Ruth's longtime friend on the general board, was killed in
an automobile accident. Called to substitute as choral director,
Ruth planned to teach only until another teacher was hired, but
she found that teaching high school music was "an immediate
love affair. I don't know when the spirit of affirmation was more
pronounced. Here again, I was able to see this generation with
their extraordinary ability to make decisions, to be leaders, to
care for one another, to govern themselves. I had noticed the
apathy of youth and their disinterest in things unless they were
truly meaningfully involved."

Each day Ruth taught five hundred students, most of whom
wanted to be involved in music activities. But she also saw a
group of problem students hanging out in the halls. She invited
their leader to play his guitar for her and to bring his friends,
and she began giving up her free period to work with them.
The boys played their guitars well, so she had them play for her
choral groups and in assembly programs, providing for most of
them their first success in high school. She maintained contact
with many of the boys after they graduated. She recalls, "It was
a privilege to work with those kids and see the unfailing spark
of divinity that's in every human being, if you just reach far
enough and accept them on their terms until they finally trust
you and know you really do like them."

A Call from a Prophet

One night Ruth had a dream that was repeated three times. In her dream, she said, "the new freeway was being built east of us, and I dreamt that I saw President Lee trying to move these enormous boulders. I was trying to help him move the boulders so the freeway could be built."

On October 27, 1972, she received a phone call at school from her husband, who told her that President Harold B. Lee wanted to meet with them after school that day. When they met in President Lee's office, he talked about the challenges of youth, particularly in the Church, and the need to strengthen the family and to develop strong youth prepared to serve in the Lord's kingdom. He then called Ruth to serve as president of the Aaronic Priesthood MIA Young Women, which would replace what had long been known as the Young Women's Mutual Improvement Association.

Ruth chose Hortense Hogan Child as first counselor and Ardeth Greene Kapp as second counselor. Ruth and Hortense had been close friends since 1949, when they met as members of the YWMIA general board. In fact, Hortense said that they were so much alike that they could share shoes and eyeglasses. Once Hortense had forgotten to change her shoes before driving to Church headquarters and still had on an old paint-splattered pair. She had to give a report at an important meeting that day, so Ruth traded shoes with her. Another time Ruth had forgotten her glasses and was asked by President Harold B. Lee, then a member of the First Presidency, to accompany the opening song at a meeting. As she walked up the aisle with her music in hand, she took Hortense's glasses off her nose, put them on, and played the hymn.[11]

Ruth, Hortense, and Ardeth had served together on the correlation committees. "Our greatest growth as far as understanding the gospel came during that time," according to Hortense.[12] Ardeth said of their correlation experience, "It helped [us] see the whole Church organization, rather than a segment of the organization. . . . It helped [us] see the Church in relation to the whole world, rather than just the Wasatch Front, as we were preparing material. As we reviewed materials, I could see

an increased emphasis on scriptural preparation in all the materials that were being written, which made what we were doing
more than just a program."[13]

On November 9, 1972, the First Presidency announced the
organization of the Melchizedek Priesthood MIA, which would
have responsibility for single adults over the age of eighteen,
and the Aaronic Priesthood MIA, which would have responsibility for youths ages twelve to eighteen. The Presiding Bishopric
would preside over the Aaronic Priesthood, assisted by the Aaronic Priesthood MIA Young Men's and Young Women's presidencies and boards. Ruth Funk and her counselors would be
responsible for programs of the Young Women, and Robert L.
Backman was appointed to head the Young Men. Presiding
Bishop Victor L. Brown explained, "The MIA under this reorganization becomes part of the priesthood and is no longer an
auxiliary."[14] At the general conference priesthood session in
April 1973, the changes were explained to the stake, ward, and
mission leaders.

As Young Women general president, Ruth had the opportunity to implement, with divine guidance, the concept of peer
leadership. "Teaching was a laboratory and a workshop for me,"
she said, "to test the theories that I believed in, but I didn't
know it at the time." As a schoolteacher, she had turned over
significant responsibilities to her students because she believed
in young people and what they could do. Both the Young Men's
and Young Women's presidencies believed that the youth should
serve in leadership capacities, with adults playing supporting
roles. Explaining the concept, Ruth said, "You give them the
opportunity to perform and to expand and magnify what gifts
they have, but the leader is there ever present to help them
become what they can become. You don't become anything by
hearing about it; you become by doing it."

President Lee had indicated in an informal meeting with
the Young Women general presidency that the concept of youth
leadership would take at least five years to implement.[15] The
years of Ruth's administration were a time for sorting out pro-
cesses and establishing procedures for restructuring the organization and providing adequate training for and communicating
with local leaders in order to establish the concept of youth

leadership. The foundation was being laid for future adminis-
trations of Young Women presidents.

At the 1973 June Conference, a new guidebook for Aaronic
Priesthood MIA leadership was introduced, outlining the structure and method by which the youth would lead themselves,
assisted by adult leaders. This was a priesthood conference
rather than an auxiliary conference, with President Lee conducting.

Over the next few years the organizational structure continued to be refined. In 1974, the Aaronic Priesthood MIA organization was restructured under the direction of the new
Church president, Spencer W. Kimball. The Aaronic Priesthood
MIA was separated into two organizations: the Aaronic Priesthood, with Rulon G. Craven as director, and the Young Women,
under general president Ruth Funk. Two years later Elder Marion
D. Hanks of the First Quorum of the Seventy was assigned to
work with the Young Women, replacing the Presiding Bishopric.
And in April 1977, the name Young Men was adopted, with Neil
D. Schaerrer called as general president.

Under the new programs, communication from the general
level to the local level underwent several changes. Bulletins to
the field were eliminated, handbooks were trimmed, and travel
was cut back so that the general board and presidency did not
conduct as many training meetings as in the past. Communications to the field were sent through the Presiding Bishopric's
office to the local priesthood leaders, who then passed information on to the auxiliary leaders, and stake leaders took greater
responsibility in training ward leaders.

At the 1975 June Conference, a heritage arts festival was
held, and each local unit was encouraged to present a similar
program the next year. The First Presidency also announced
that June Conference would be discontinued and replaced by
regional conferences in order, as President Kimball said, to "take
the program to the people."[16] To encourage local units to become more self-reliant in meeting their own needs, scripts and
musical programs produced on the general level were no longer
printed and sent out. At first many stake and ward leaders felt
they couldn't produce their own programs, but they soon found
their efforts not only effective but, according to one leader,

"better than June Conference." Ardeth Kapp observed as she
traveled around the Church that the program of youth assuming
greater leadership roles was beginning to work effectively in
areas where the concept was understood and practiced.[17]

During Ruth Funk's administration, the Young Womanhood
Recognition program, emphasizing inner growth, goal setting,
service, and accountability, replaced the girls' program. In 1974,
the general presidency published "Behold Thy Handmaiden,"
which introduced six areas of focus for young women: spiritual
awareness, homemaking arts, service and compassion, recreation and the world of nature, cultural arts and education, and
personal and social refinement. Each girl who worked on goals
she set in her own "My Personal Progress" booklet received a
yearly certificate of progress. Laurels, at the end of their first
year and as a culmination of their years in Young Women, were
eligible to receive the Young Womanhood Recognition award
by meeting standards of personal worthiness, attendance at
church meetings, and achieving two goals in each area of focus
for each year of membership in the Young Women program.

Because of Ruth's great interest in music, the Young Women
published a songbook, *Songs of the Heart,* to provide music that
was both uplifting and appealing. Three manuals were also published for the Beehive, Mia Maid, and Laurel age groups.

In December 1977, Ruth discussed with President Spencer
W. Kimball the possibility of having a meeting, similar to general
priesthood meetings, for the young women of the Church. Preparations continued through the first half of the year for that
historic meeting, which was scheduled to be held in the Salt
Lake Tabernacle in September 1978. That May President Kimball
called Ruth into his office and expressed his gratitude for all
that she and her counselors in the Young Women presidency
had done during the five and a half years they had served and
said they were now to be released. The releases were publicly
announced July 12.

Following their release, Ardeth Kapp wrote in her journal,
"I think of the great and noble women that I have been privileged
to work with, of whom it will be said, when the history of the
Young Women from 1972 to 1978 is opened and read, 'Who
else could have sustained the trauma of three major organiza-

tional changes, three changes of the Young Men's presidency, three changes of location, and three changes of priesthood advisors or managing directors?' "[18]

Hortense Child, Ruth's counselor and friend for more than forty years, said of Ruth: "The things I admire most about her are her absolute and complete optimism, her unconditional love, her capacity for insight into people, and her great efforts for service toward each and every one that comes along. She is totally dedicated to doing good. She has also contributed greatly to the culture of the Church with her elevation of music and her sensitivity to the cultural heritage of the Church."[19]

Released but Not Retired

After the Funk children grew up, married, and began having children, Ruth and Marcus added a room on the back of their home to provide additional space for family gatherings. Family activities have remained important to the Funks, just as they were when their four children were growing up. Now the family circle has expanded with the grandchildren.

"My children have loved going to their grandmother's house because she gets involved with them and plays games with them," says Nancy. "When they were young, one of the activities they enjoyed most was dancing around her living room while she played the piano. If they wanted to be butterflies, she would play butterfly music. If they wanted to be ogres, she would play ogre music. She has always been very interested in her grandchildren and what is going on in their lives."[20] On each grandchild's birthday, Ruth takes the child on a "Grandma date." They go to a restaurant selected by the child, and then they go shopping so the birthday honoree can choose a special present. When a grandchild acquires a driver's license, Ruth drives to that young adult's home and asks the new driver to take her for a ride.

In addition to family activities, Ruth has found other ways to serve. Soon after her release from Young Women, she was called as the spiritual living teacher in her ward's Relief Society. For the sesquicentennial of the Church in 1980, she and George I. Cannon coproduced *Zion*, a musical production. In 1983,

George, then serving as Ruth's stake president, asked her to direct *Zion* in the Parley's Stake; 40 percent of the stake members participated. For the 140th anniversary of Relief Society in 1982, Barbara B. Smith, general president of the Relief Society, asked Ruth to serve as coordinator for a series of concerts, featuring outstanding LDS women, in Salt Lake City, Dallas, Washington, D.C., and Oakland and Los Angeles, California.

Throughout Ruth's life, she has been involved in community service with such organizations as PTA, the Cancer Society, American Red Cross, United Fund, Utah Symphony Guild, American Association of Women, National Federation of Music, Music Circle, Piano Club, and University of Utah Alumni Association. For fifteen years she was on the board of directors of Promised Valley Playhouse. She was an elected delegate from Utah to the 1977 International Women's Year convention in Houston, Texas, and served on the National and International Councils of Women. She was chairman of the Governor's Commission on the Status of Women, and has been a member of the board of directors of Bonneville International Corporation. For eight years she served as a member and then as chairman of the Utah State Board of Education.

Ruth has received many honors and awards, including the 1991 Distinguished Alumnus Award from the University of Utah, Woman of Achievement from the Utah Federation of Business and Professional Women, Distinguished Service to Public Education, Kiwanis Teacher of the Month, and Bonneville International Corporation Presidential Citation for Excellence.

Marcus retired from his dental practice in 1985, and both he and Ruth have suffered in recent years from a series of health problems. Ruth became blind in one eye and has macrodegeneration and a cataract in the other eye and glaucoma in both of them, which she termed as "her greatest trial." "We laugh about who is supposed to take care of whom," she says.

In spite of her visual difficulties, Ruth, with her usual undaunted spirit, still approaches life with enthusiasm and determination. In October 1990, she and her daughter Allyson, along with her brother Grant, visited areas where her ancestors lived in England because, as Ruth said, "Genealogy is one of the things I haven't done."

"I marvel as I look back at the divine orchestration of my life," she reflects. "I really do believe that the Lord customizes our experiences according to our needs. The gospel is the vehicle whereby almost every life you touch is touched and changed in some miraculous sort of way for good if you allow the Holy Ghost to lead you. But I think you have to give up your own independence and become totally dependent on the Lord to maximize your ultimate blessings or to be able to give ultimately to anyone. I feel the Lord expects us to go as far as we can with what he has given us. But I know that I cannot do what I need to do or must do until I finally come to him in total dependence."

Ruth Hardy Funk's life has been filled with music and young people through her family life, her professional work, and her church callings. Because she has willingly redirected her talents and followed the course she believes the Lord wants for her, she has truly been an instrument in his hands.

8

Elaine Cannon
1978–1984

*T*he mixer whirred as Elaine Cannon stood in her kitchen one March afternoon making a cake for her wedding anniversary. Unable to hear the screams of her little girls over the sounds of the mixer, she felt the prompting of the Holy Ghost telling her to go to the pond. Immediately, she ran out of the house to a deep pond near their home. When she reached it, she found three-year-old Susan with her arms through the fence holding on to four-year-old Christine's hand. Christine had slipped on the soft spring snow as she tried to get a ball that had bounced onto the rough rocks at the pond's edge. Though Christine suffered scratches and cuts, Elaine saved her from drowning.[1]

Listening to the Spirit has always been important to Elaine Anderson Cannon, eighth general president of the Young Women, whether she is facing a challenge in her personal life or facing an audience of eager young women in her public life. "I have cultivated my relationship with the Holy Ghost," she says. "I have yearned after guidance, warning, and inspiration from him. I have watched for it and heeded it. Promptings from the Spirit have been one of the great blessings of my life."

"Let Me Soar!"[2]

Filled with a hearty love for life and people, Elaine found magic in the Capitol Hill neighborhood in which she grew up in Salt Lake City. She was born April 9, 1922, the second child of Aldon J. and Minnie Egan Anderson. She had an older brother,

Aldon, Jr., and a younger brother and sister, Lowell and Nadine. Her childhood was filled with riding the stone lions on the stairs of the Utah State Capitol in the long, warm shadows of a late summer evening, leading childish parades over steep neighborhood hills, directing costumed pageants in her garage on a hot afternoon, and counting the stars in a moonless winter sky. The simple experiences of life on Capitol Hill grew into significant lessons of life that gave her wisdom and optimism even as a child. From the capitol gardener who showed her that plants always turned toward the light, she learned to look to the giver of life; and from a bitter woman who unjustly criticized her, she learned about hate and hypocrisy. She emerged from her childhood ready to soar skyward.

Elaine had to look no further than her parents and grandparents for examples of spirituality. Her paternal grandmother, Elise Holter, embraced the gospel in Norway when she was seventeen years old and immigrated to Salt Lake City, where she met and married a young Swedish inventor, Per Anderson. They became the parents of ten children.

Elaine's mother was a descendant of faithful Latter-day Saint pioneers, including Ezra Taft Benson, Sr., who was ordained an apostle in 1846, and Major Howard Egan, a pony express rider. Her maternal grandparents, Horace and Evaline Benson Egan, reared their family of seven children in Idaho and Utah.

Minnie Egan Anderson, Elaine's mother, was as comfortable feeding a hobo on her back porch during the Depression as she was serving on the YWMIA general board. "I learned to drink deeply of life from my mother," Elaine has written. "Mother used to give us a hug and remark, 'The teachers have you all winter. Come summer, you're mine.' "[3] The children enjoyed a wide variety of activities with their mother each summer. They cooked breakfast over a campfire, learned how to swim in the Great Salt Lake without inhaling the salt water, and held summer Primary in their garage while the Capitol Hill Ward meetinghouse was under construction.

According to Minnie, Elaine had a mania in her early years for organizing clubs—sewing clubs, athletic clubs, and social clubs. "I was never surprised to see Elaine coming home from school leading several little girls, who then came trooping into our living room, ready to have a club meeting. The organization would take place in a most formal manner. Officers were always elected, then Elaine would give a talk. The peculiar thing about the election was that somehow Elaine was always chosen president and her best friend was always made secretary. Elaine kept a separate notebook filled with meticulous notes for each club."[4]

Elaine recalls her wonder that her mother constantly worked to improve herself, including teaching herself how to play the piano and violin and to speak French. Minnie provided her children with a wide range of opportunities — not only formal training in speech, but also exposure to art, music, and drama.

Elaine and her father also shared a close relationship. "My father thought everything we children did was marvelous," she says. "You can imagine what that did to build confidence in me as a young girl! There was love, love, love. I became comfortable praying to my Heavenly Father very early because I felt my earthly father and my Heavenly Father must be very much alike."

One of the many lessons Elaine learned from her father came as a result of her innocent childhood mistake of painting the petals of an oleander that had been a gift from her grandmother. She later wrote of the incident and the lesson she learned from it: " 'One cannot improve on God,' Daddy declared emphatically. . . . The oleander died, of course, but Daddy's counsel lives in me yet. A chair can be repainted to cover past damages, but a living, growing thing can be spoiled forever through witless tampering. And that goes for people as well as plants."[5]

An ability to get along with people and a talent for writing both surfaced early in Elaine's life. In junior high school she was instrumental in starting a school paper. During her senior year she started writing a high school report for the Salt Lake *Telegram*. This was the beginning of her long career as a daily newspaper columnist — three years for the *Telegram* and more than twenty-five years for the *Deseret News*.

Elaine entered the University of Utah in the fall of 1939, majoring in sociology. Charismatic and fun, she was busy and popular in college, even being named the "Dream Girl" of a fraternity. She served as president of the Associated Women

Students and of Chi Omega sorority, was a member of the University of Utah women's vocal sextet, and was elected to Mortar Board and Beehive honor societies.

Her activities were not all centered around academics and work. Her leadership skills were put to use in the University Ward as president of the Young Women's Mutual Improvement Association, where she shared her dynamic gifts of optimism and spirituality. She was campus columnist for the university's paper, the *Daily Utah Chronicle,* and continued to write and serve as assistant woman's editor for the *Telegram.*

"Because of my column in the society section, I had free tickets to everything," Elaine says, describing one of the perks of her newspaper work. "This was the era of the Big Bands. Since money was tight during these late depression and early World War II years, friends would say 'Let's call Elaine.' They did and we'd go to Saltair, Lagoon, the Starlight Gardens of Hotel Utah, or the Rainbow," some of the most popular dance halls in the area. Although she had many beaux, it was D. James Cannon who won her heart.

Marriage and Family Life

When Jim Cannon met Elaine, he was a student at the University of Utah and a fraternity brother of Elaine's brother Aldon. A son of Sylvester Q. Cannon, a member of the Quorum of the Twelve who had previously served as Presiding Bishop, and Winifred I. Saville, Jim spent his early years in the Cannon farm area on the west side of Salt Lake City. After he graduated from the University of Utah in 1940, he served a mission to Hawaii. Though he and Elaine had known each other for five years, they didn't date seriously until after he returned from his mission. They were married in the Salt Lake Temple on Thursday, March 25, 1943, between quarters of Elaine's senior year. The following Monday, she became editor of the society and women's pages of the *Deseret News,* a job she held for a year and a half. Two months after her marriage, she graduated from the University of Utah.

Jim and Elaine had six children, two sons and four daughters. Their four oldest children, James, Carla, Christine, and

Susan, were born at about fourteen-month intervals. Holly joined the family two years after Susan, and Anthony was born four years later. "My children are stalwarts, but I can't take credit for that," Elaine says. "They are choice spirits. My children are stars in their own sphere." However, she and Jim are happy to take credit for strict upbringing and for striving to enrich their children's lives through gospel, cultural, and service-oriented experiences. Both Jim's career in public relations and Elaine's career as a journalist brought rich dimensions of the world to their family.

"As a child, I can remember that dinner time was a time for interesting conversation," recalls Tony. "We didn't talk about surface or shallow kinds of things either. Dad was good about asking us what we thought about news events or teaching us about the holidays in detail. He was also good with facts and quizzes. When we'd go on trips, for example, he'd ask us the name of the longest river or the highest mountain in Utah."[6]

Holidays provided a time for fun and for teaching moments. On Memorial Day the family would visit the cemetery in the morning and then go on a picnic. On July 24, they would go to the Days of '47 parade downtown, then visit "This Is the Place Monument" to honor the pioneers who had arrived in the Salt Lake Valley on that day in 1847. Even moving into a new home had its own traditions. Whenever the family moved, they had family prayer and dedicated their home. Each person took a turn in the prayer to express his or her hopes and what he or she wanted to accomplish while living in this home. After Christine's near drowning, the Cannons were grateful that they had dedicated not only their home but also the pond that no one would lose his or her life in it.

Family conversations, happy summers at Elaine's parents' cabin on Hebgen Lake near Yellowstone National Park, and a mutual love and respect for one another helped keep the family close. These relationships have aided them as they have met challenges. Jim's unsuccessful political campaigns for Utah governor in 1964 and Salt Lake City mayor in 1967 put great demands on the family in terms of time, money, and stress. Though the political climate was not favorable for him, the family learned to pull together. "Elaine was a brick through it all," Jim says. "I had to take a leave of absence from my job as director of the state travel commission both times I made a political bid, so I had no income during that time."[7] Tony remembers that each family member was involved in the campaigns and that Jim and Elaine "helped the rest of us through even though it was probably harder on them than it was on us."[8]

Jim and Elaine have always supported one another. "Jim has been a great blessing to me," she says. "He has turned me loose when opportunities have come my way, and he has been an insightful priesthood support. He says, 'Sure, you can do it.' " In turn, she consistently supported him during the times he served as a bishop and on the high councils of two stakes, and in other church, community, and business-related activities. Her church callings during the early years of their marriage utilized her energy and creativity as a member of a stake YWMIA board and as director for several roadshows. They also shared parental responsibilities. Often Jim played with the children, taking them on sleigh rides or helping them build snowmen during the day, and singing them to sleep at night. When Elaine was sewing or cooking, she enjoyed having her children read or talk to her, and she took turns reading to them too.

"Mom was a loyal parent," remembers Jamie. "She listened to us and wanted to know how we perceived experiences and how we felt, not just what we did. Yet she was a stern taskmaster with high expectations for us."[9]

Elaine's excellent skills with people and her firm relationship with Christ have added a strong spiritual dimension to her mothering. "My mother is the most highly spiritual woman I know," says her daughter Susan. "She turns to the gospel for answers at every juncture. She lives it every day and applies its principles in every situation. As a mother she was absolutely firm in her commitment to do it the Lord's way. She gave us, therefore, the greatest gift a mother can give—she loved us enough to thoroughly teach us the gospel of Jesus Christ."[10]

Writing and Mothering

"I stayed home with my children when they were small," Elaine says, "but I never missed a daily column in twenty-five years. I used to get up at 4:00 a.m. and write my column before the baby's six o'clock feeding."[11] In 1947, when she had three small children, she began writing a *Deseret News* column, "Hi Tales," for teenagers. All of her children remember the continuous rolls of paper with attached triplicate carbons on which she typed her columns. "I remember her tearing off chunks of it," says Jamie. "Then we would jump in the car and race down to the old Richards Street entrance of the *Deseret News*. My job was to run it up to the third floor because Mom couldn't always find a parking place."[12]

"Some of my earliest memories are of sitting on Mom's lap while she was typing," says Tony. "I remember watching her hands fly over the keyboard. And I loved drawing with her dark number two pencils while she was working. In spite of the fact that she was very involved with things like that, she was good about making time for us. I never felt slighted."[13]

Opportunities came often to talented Elaine, and somehow she managed to juggle them all. In 1949 she began her first weekly television show, which lasted for many years. She worked as a freelance reporter for *Seventeen* and *Better Homes and Gardens*. As a columnist for the *Deseret News*, she often interviewed celebrities who came to town.

When Elaine came up with the idea of having an annual back-to-school fashion show for young women, she was a busy young mother of three and still writing her daily column, and her husband was serving as a bishop. "Seminar for Sallies," as the fashion show was known, was sponsored by the *Deseret News* and attracted more than one thousand young people that first year, in August 1948. The annual production featured skits on topics of interest to teenagers and young women modeling back-to-school fashions. Elaine was involved with every detail, from writing the script to building the scenery and narrating the show. Eventually the program included young men, and the name was changed to "Seminar for Sallies and Sams." Similar seminars were produced in other Utah cities, in Idaho, and as far away as Halifax, Vancouver, Boston, and London. The last one was produced in 1970, twenty-three years after the program began.

Awards and honors began to come to Elaine also, including

an appointment as a delegate to the White House Conference on Children and Youth, a citation from *Seventeen* for her work with youth, and first-place honors in writing and editing competitions sponsored by the National Federation of Press Women.

Though Elaine's activities and writings gave her a high profile in the community, she was able to maintain a balance in her home between being a wife and mother and having a career. After she entertained, the children would entertain their friends the next day while the linen, candles, and flowers were still in place; thus, when they helped her prepare for her parties, they were getting things ready for their parties too.

Elaine recognized that while many demands were placed on her during these mothering years, they also allowed her to help with the family finances. "I think the Lord knew I could be trusted to keep my family first," she says. "You can't maintain a heavy schedule unless your heart is in the right place, or you'll end up with broken hearts."

Elaine's busy life took on new dimensions in 1959 when she, her mother, and her brother Aldon opened a fabric store, The Dressmaker. They specialized in selling fine fabrics, buttons, braids, and yarns, including many imported items that were new to Salt Lake City. This venture was an extension of a talent Elaine had for decorating or redecorating. "A new facelift on the walls and furniture lifted mother's spirits," according to her daughter Susan. "She did all the paper hanging, painting, and upholstering herself. We have all learned to do the same — to make the most out of what we have to work with."[14]

The same year The Dressmaker opened, Elaine also became the associate editor of a new "Era of Youth" section in the *Improvement Era*. Elder Marion D. Hanks, at that time a member of the First Council of the Seventy, was the editor of the monthly section. As a team, they motivated the youth of the Church with the written word in the colorful and dynamic "Era of Youth." Elaine, with her sparkle and vibrant love of people, and Elder Hanks, with his distinctively resonant speaking voice and teaching ability, captivated audiences wherever they spoke.

The popularity of the section over the next ten years grew steadily, and eventually it led to an entire magazine for youth — the *New Era*. Elaine, who had ties with *Seventeen*, made arrangements for those involved in planning the new magazine to visit publishers of several youth magazines in New York City, where they saw what the world was doing for young people and why the Church needed an alternative voice. "Probably the one person in the world who did the most to perpetuate a magazine for youth was Elaine Cannon," Elder Hanks recalls. "Because of her, we were well prepared when we made our presentation [for a new magazine] to President Spencer W. Kimball, then the President of the Quorum of the Twelve."[15]

After listening to the group's presentation, Elaine says, "President Kimball put his fist down and said, 'Let's do it and I'll get the first subscription.' " In 1971 the Church began publishing the the *New Era* for young people.

Elaine gave up her daily newspaper column to help to establish the *New Era.* She also was called to serve as the national advisor to women for the LDS Student Association. As part of that assignment, she helped to establish a sorority for college-age women, Lambda Delta Sigma, while Rolfe Kerr, the executive secretary of LDSSA, directed the establishment of a fraternity for college-age men, Sigma Gamma Chi.

Always interested in women's issues, Elaine attended the International Women's Conference in Houston, Texas, in 1976 with Florence S. Jacobsen and Young Women president Ruth Hardy Funk. Unrest filled many women as America struggled with the decision of whether or not to pass the Equal Rights Amendment (ERA) to the Constitution. "Elaine was very strong for women's understanding of their potentiality," remembers Jim. "She believed in the God-given roles of priesthood and womanhood and spent a lot of time presenting this viewpoint to others."[16]

A Helping Friend

In her book *The Summer of My Content*, published in 1976, Elaine wrote of a turning point in her lifelong commitment to Christ:

"At seventeen I felt very grown-up. I was about to have my patriarchal blessing. . . . The night before my appointment with Patriarch Jones I felt a strong need to gather myself together with Heavenly Father. I went quickly out the screened door and stood there for a time listening to the summers of my youth sift by on the night song of the crickets. Then I felt once again the pull of the stars. Shyly at first I lay down on my back on prickly grass as I had done so often as a child. Once again I took a deep breath and turned my face skyward. . . . I studied the heavens, finding the familiar constellations, getting placement with the North Star. Then finally, the mind-stretching, soul-searing experience of being lifted into the universe — almost into the presence of God — set my heart to pounding. My prayers that night got through. The witness of the Spirit that God lives and cares and was mindful of little me warmed me to tears."[17]

"Elaine is truly a disciple of Christ," says Elder Hanks, who has been friends with her since they were in junior high school. "She was very popular in high school and college — the president of nearly everything and the queen of the ball — but these things are really secondary to her commitment to the Lord. She is a true servant and has always lived that way."[18]

This spiritual depth would ultimately become apparent in her writing, her speaking, and her leadership style. "I have been to Gethsemane and Galilee," she said in 1981. "I have bowed my head at Golgotha. I have wept in the Garden Tomb near Jerusalem. I have studied the scriptural accounts and heard the testimonies of prophets. And I have my own witness as well — Christ lives!"[19]

Elaine's relationship with people usually works on two levels: "let's have fun" and "let's talk." "She won't miss anything that's exciting," says Winnifred Jardine, a former food editor for the *Deseret News* and Elaine's longtime friend. "She loves life and makes it fun for everybody around her. Her charisma intrigues and fascinates everyone. All eyes are drawn to her in any kind of a group. Yet she never comes to anything empty handed; she always contributes to every good time."[20]

"People were always coming to the house for counsel," remembers Holly. "Even after their life crisis passed, they sought her as a friend. Household help, egg man, milk man, grocer, cleaners, the church maintenance person — all became mother's friends. They were important to her."[21]

"You can't say I'm an expert at anything except at loving

people," Elaine claims. "I'm so interested in people, and I do ache for everybody who is suffering." In one of her books she wrote, "People always have affected me deeply one way or the other, chilling or warming my sensitive soul either by their suffering or their joy, or mine."[22] She has lived her life immersed in the lives of other people and their joys and challenges. She is not only an optimist herself, but a weaver of optimism and hope into the lives of others.

One of Jim and Elaine Cannon's most painful challenges was the death of Jamie's wife Christine Jacobsen Cannon, who died of cancer in January 1975, leaving Jamie and three small sons. "Mom helped us in two ways," says Jamie. "She cared for our sons for several months when Christine was in the hospital, and she constantly slipped me notes or cards with gems of insight from her endless supply of quotes. These really helped me keep an eternal perspective on everything that was happening to us. And beyond that, it was Mom who eventually introduced me to Becky, my new wife."[23]

Leader of Young Women

Through the years, most of Elaine's service in the Church centered around youth and writing. She served in YWMIA ward and stake presidencies, on the YWMIA general board, and on the Church's correlation and instructional development committees. She wrote lessons for gospel doctrine and Relief Society manuals, organized productions presented at June Conference, and was co-chair of the Church's American Bicentennial committee and executive secretary of the Church's sesquicentennial celebration. Yet she was still surprised that she would be called as Young Women president at the age of fifty-six. She quipped that "it was like getting pregnant at fifty."[24] But it was the combination of her love for and understanding of young people and her strong testimony that qualified her for this calling as much as her experience and organizational skills.

Strong impressions prepared her for the call five weeks before it came. When she told President Spencer W. Kimball of this spiritual preparation, she recalls, he said, "This is a gift. Always remember it is the Lord who wants you in this calling, not just me. This spiritual preparation is a gift, and there will be times when this knowledge will be a blessing to you."

On July 12, 1978, the First Presidency officially announced Elaine's appointment as president of the Young Women, with Arlene B. Darger and Norma B. Smith as her counselors. She pledged to rely upon the Lord as she made decisions for the Young Women, explaining, "I am very much aware that this is not *my* program, and so I must always try to know what the Lord wants me to do."[25]

Elaine and her counselors were in charge of the first general women's meeting, held in the Salt Lake Tabernacle in September 1978. The general presidents of the Relief Society and Primary were invited to speak, and a chorus of girls, young women, and women sang. "It was an exciting giant step forward, underlining the specific and inspired continuum of woman's place in the Church," Elaine said.

Under Elaine's leadership, the general board was reduced from sixty members to twelve. "Every board member had a daughter of Young Women age," recalls Winnifred Jardine, one of the board members. "The young women served as ad hoc members of the board and were used as a sounding board."[26] To make full use of the smaller board, each member was given an area of responsibility and worked with women who were called as needed to help plan and direct the various programs.

"Prepare to Perform" became the leadership theme for the YWMIA board. At their weekly meetings they were taught out of the scriptures by General Authorities, received training from experts in communications, and learned international protocol, all designed to help them to effectively present themselves and the gospel throughout the world.

"Elaine is a great administrator and a complex personality," says counselor Norma Smith. "Some days she was at her efficient best, some days at her spiritual best, some days at her fun-loving best, and some days at her compassionate best, but most days she was all these and more."[27]

Under Elaine's leadership, the board continued working toward the goal of simplifying the Young Women program, yet building upon traditions from the past, such as reinstituting the singing of "Carry On," popular in the YWMIA since Ruth May

Fox wrote the lyrics in 1930, and the practice of repeating the spiritual theme each week. Special activities often grew out of gospel principles. For the sesquicentennial of the Church in 1980, each young woman was invited to create her own personal banner. This activity, like many of the things that happened during Elaine's administration, was inspired by one of her childhood experiences. One June morning, when she was sixteen, she had climbed Ensign Peak north of her home on the northern edge of Salt Lake City alone and looked down upon her neighborhood. She later described her feelings:

"This day my aloneness was exhilarating as I made my way to the top. . . . I sat looking down at the houses I knew so well and at their people beginning to stir with the sun. . . . I watched the achingly familiar scenes as an extension of myself. Yet, it was like being God, seeing the whole picture. Seeing but not being seen. . . . In 1847 Brigham Young had raised an ensign to the Lord on this peak, according to the plaque on top. Well, I raised my own that day and came down from the mount determined to be useful."[28]

When the Young Women made their banners, they too had to think about their standards before God as they painted, appliquéd, or embroidered onto their banners designs that represented the beliefs that guided their lives and their feelings for the Lord. One thousand young women dressed in white and carrying their banners mounted on tall staffs marched in Salt Lake City's Days of '47 parade. Local units throughout the Church had their own banner events.

"Elaine has an incredible will to carry on in the grand style," says Laurel Bailey, her personal secretary for many years. "She simply will not be less than what she is at her best."[29]

A longtime advocate of spiritual growth for young people, Elaine was pleased when the consolidated meeting schedule, adopted churchwide in 1980, provided a time for young women to attend church at the same time as the Aaronic Priesthood classes were held and to have comparable spiritual lessons. Flexibility in the design of the new manuals allowed each teacher to prayerfully choose those lessons that seemed most applicable to the concerns and needs of the members of her class. Special weekday activities, which encouraged service, grew out of the Sunday instruction.

On a general Church level, other changes were developing during Elaine's administration. The three presidencies of the Relief Society, Young Women, and Primary began holding joint meetings and traveling together on assignments to the field. Another change involved the alignment of some procedures involving the programs for young women and young men. For example, bishops began to interview young women as they turned twelve and to advance them from Primary to Young Women at that time, just as boys reaching twelve moved on to the Aaronic Priesthood and the Young Men's program.

For Elaine, people have always been more important than programs. When she was twelve, she wrote in her journal, "I want to remember experiences that I am having at this age, so I will know how to help young women when I grow up."[30]

Always very much in demand as a youth speaker, she often spoke at firesides, standards nights, and youth conferences. "Elaine is a real presence," observes Elder Hanks. "She has this rare combination of abilities—intelligence, perception, and sensitivity—but it is her total effect that is so powerful. As Young Women president, she radiated a genuine concern, interest, and love for the young women. Her leadership was inspired and she had the ability to excite them. The young women used to flock around her like the Pied Piper, and so did the leaders. It was an honor to be a friend of Elaine Cannon."[31]

Jamie noted a change in his mother after she began to visit young women outside the United States, particularly in underdeveloped countries. "Mom recognized the challenges in the lives of these young women and how different they were from young women growing up in affluent American homes," says Jamie. "She developed a great desire to have the Young Women's program be spiritually rewarding for all the young women. I think that really affected the way she approached the program."[32]

Leaders of the Relief Society and the Young Women had long been active in both the National Council of Women and the International Council of Women. Carrying on this tradition, Elaine served a two-year term as a vice-president of the five-million-member NCW/USA. She was honored in 1984 at the

NCW's awards ceremony for "her ability to communicate with young people and their families without losing her role as representative of old-fashioned, solid values."[33]

As a leader of the home economics committee of the International Council of Women, Elaine had many opportunities to suggest gospel principles as solutions to worldwide problems. For instance, at a workshop in Korea where the problems of abortion, family break-up, and venereal disease were discussed, she suggested chastity as a solution. The reaction of the committee members was blank stares. When one woman asked, "What's chastity?" Elaine obligingly provided a definition.[34] "I didn't directly try to sell the Church, but I did hard-sell the principles of the gospel," she says. "They are the answers to the world's problems."[35]

Life after Young Women

After Elaine was released as president of the Young Women on April 7, 1984, her life did not slow down—it only changed direction. She found more time to write, though her writing had never really stopped. She has written more than thirty books on subjects ranging from adversity to writing your life story. She has written text for coloring books, baptism books for eight-year-olds, and motivational books for young adults. She maintains that she is not a gifted writer, but has simply been blessed by the Lord with ideas and rich life experiences. She still often gets up at four o'clock to write, and readily acknowledges that she is a hard worker and that she "simply loves it."

Twenty-five grandchildren, including two sets of identical twins, are also a big part of Elaine's life. Her relationship with them alternates between cheerful moments filled with laughter and serious moments filled with spiritual insights. For example, one night as Elaine and her grandson Peter sat watching the stars, Peter asked, "Are the stars there every time it gets dark, even if I can't see them?" She assured him that they were, even behind the clouds. "Darkness isn't so bad, is it?" she said, adding, "If you know the stars are there."[36]

"Attitude in adversity turns hopeless to hopeful," Elaine said in a general women's meeting in 1982.[37] She spoke from experience. All her life, she has been plagued with a wide variety of health problems, yet she has found the strength to cheerfully move ahead with her life. At seventeen she won a jitterbug contest shortly after an appendectomy—and despite the fact that she had a drain tube in her. Pain from imbedded teeth didn't keep her from being in the school play, and serious foot surgery didn't stop her from school activities—it only slowed her down.

From the constant stomachaches she suffered as a child to the rare disease of the arteries she battles now, nothing has dimmed her optimism. Through surgeries, infections, a cracked vertebra in her neck, heart problems, and a variety of other physical ailments, she has continued to laugh, raise her family, inspire friends, work hard, and lead and comfort others. "When I ask her how she is feeling," according to Jim, "she always answers 'I'll be better tomorrow.' "[38]

"These are nuisances for me," adds Elaine, who on several occasions took a portable typewriter with her to the hospital so she could meet deadline schedules. "I'm a lively person who won't stay down. I have finally come to believe that I have been blessed having these challenges. They have increased my humility, my empathy for others, and my faith in Christ. I've had a couple of close calls, but I have had priesthood blessings that literally saved my life."

"With an apparent inability to whimper, Elaine meets her challenges with dignity and integrity," Elder Hanks says. "I believe she copes with her pain through faith, an indomitable will, and incredible courage. She will not be defeated."[39]

Shortly before Elaine's release as general president of Young Women, Jim had a heart attack. Three years later, as they were preparing to move to St. George in southern Utah, he suffered a stroke, which was followed by additional strokes, and he has had to be confined to a wheelchair.

For more than a year Elaine and Jim's second daughter, Christine, suffered from a rare disease that required long hospital stays. Elaine traveled between St. George and Salt Lake City often so she could be with her and help to care for her two children, Abby and Jake. Elaine often did a "blessing count" with her daughter to help her remember all the good things she still had in life. With her mother at her bedside, Christine died in December 1991. She was buried in the Salt Lake City cemetery beside Jamie's wife Christine Jacobsen Cannon, who also died as a young mother.

After Elaine and Jim moved to St. George, Carla visited them about once a month to help them with errands and chores. She and Elaine enjoyed planning a garden that would survive in that desert setting, and spent many happy hours visiting nurseries in search of flowering plants and the right ground cover for the slope behind the house. "These joyful memories will stay with me forever," Carla said. "Children don't often have the chance to see their parents from this new perspective."[40]

Throughout her life Elaine has been an avid journal keeper. She is fond of saying, "A life recorded is a life twice lived."[41] In recent years she and Jim have compiled their personal histories, and they have encouraged their children and grandchildren to record their experiences and feelings in journals.

In 1981 at a Young Women conference in Germany, Elaine spoke to the theme "You Can Soar." Her words summarize her life: "You can soar if you find out who you are and why you are here. There are two important days in a woman's life: the day she is born and the day she finds out why. I firmly believe there is something each one of us must do. If we don't do it, it doesn't get done. It's such an exciting thing to prepare oneself to make a difference in the world."

Elaine Cannon has made a difference in the world. She has filled the air with laughter, mended broken hearts, inspired family and friends, led young women, and written words of encouragement. She knows why she is here, she is doing what she must do, and she herself has soared.

9

Ardeth Greene Kapp
1984–1992

*I*n November 1985, early in her administration as ninth general president of Young Women, Ardeth Greene Kapp addressed the young women and said: "I see the crest of a great wave forming. As I look back over the history of the young women in the Church, I marvel at each swell of accomplishment. Yet I see a wave forming that will move across the earth, reaching every continent and every shore. I call upon you to stand with me to prepare to take your place in a great forward movement among the young women of the Church — a movement in which you are destined to shape history and participate in the fulfillment of prophecy."[1]

Sister Kapp stood at the crest of a great forward movement in the history of the Young Women. She led out in a sure direction because she is a woman of vision.

Strong Roots and a Memorable Childhood

Ardeth Kapp's ancestors settled in southern Alberta, Canada, as a direct result of their faith and commitment to The Church of Jesus Christ of Latter-day Saints. Her paternal great-great-grandfather, John Portineus Greene, married Rhoda Young, Brigham Young's sister. John was a close friend of the Prophet Joseph Smith and served as the marshal in Nauvoo, Illinois. Evan Melbourne Greene, her great-grandfather, married Susan Kent Young, a niece of Brigham Young. He assisted in building the Kirtland Temple, attended the School of the Prophets, and was present when section 84 of the Doctrine and Covenants, a revelation on the priesthood, was given to Joseph Smith. Daniel Kent Greene, Ardeth's grandfather, married after returning from a mission and settled in Aetna, Alberta, Canada. In 1913, he plowed the first furrow to break ground for the Alberta Temple in Cardston.

Ardeth's maternal great-great-grandparents, Jeremiah and Sarah Studevant Leavitt, moved from New Hampshire to Quebec, Canada, in the early 1800s. There they heard of the restored gospel, but they were not baptized until they moved to Kirtland, Ohio. The Leavitts began their exodus from Nauvoo to the Salt Lake Valley in 1846, farming along the way to replenish their food supply. Jeremiah died in Iowa, and Sarah and her children continued the journey to Utah. Ardeth's great-grandfather, Thomas R. Leavitt, and her grandfather, Edwin Jenkins Leavitt, helped settle southern Alberta in 1890.

Ardeth Greene was born in Cardston March 19, 1931, the third child of Edwin (Ted) Kent and Julia (June) Leavitt Greene. Her older sister, Uvada, died as an infant. She has an older brother, Gordon Kay, and two younger sisters, Sharon and Shirley Mae. "My father and mother were yoked together as a great team," Ardeth says. "They had differences, but great strengths and a unity in purpose that has had a profound impact on my life."

The Greene family suffered the effects of the Great Depression, as did many other families in the Cardston area. Ted sold all but eighty acres of his land, and the family moved from the farm to the town of Glenwood, ten miles northwest of Cardston on the vast Canadian prairie. To help the family economy, June opened a one-room general store that, as Ardeth remembers, "had everything from mousetraps to English bone china to vinegar to ready-to-wear dresses to overalls and rubber boots and a gas pump." As soon as Ardeth was tall enough to see over the counter, she helped her mother in the store.

"My mom ran this little store with all the dignity and the professionalism that you would expect in the finest store in the country," Ardeth remembers. "No matter what the weather was, she opened the store on time. No matter what the circumstances were, she never closed a minute early for fear a customer would come. She treated every customer with the same dignity you would expect for the most important person. Many of our customers were the Indians from the Blood Indian Reservation and residents from the Hutterite colony, besides all of the farmers and people in the surrounding community.

"The thing I remember most about my mom was that when people would come in and didn't have money to pay for their groceries, she would let them charge them until they got their paychecks. The Indians often didn't get their checks until the end of the month, but she carried them. She loved children and would keep track of the ones who came into the store and send them notes and cards. She was unbelievably patient while the children took ever so long selecting their penny candies from the wide variety available."

June was not, by circumstance or nature, the "traditional kind of mother," according to Ardeth. "I don't ever remember that she had hot cookies in the oven when I came home from school, but I remember that I worked beside her and that I saw her put store-bought cookies into the bags of people who couldn't afford them. I don't remember her reading stories to me, but I remember that she started the first lending library in our town of 300 people. Mother loved to read and bought a few good books and loaned them out for ten cents a book. Many people were able to read good books because she started a lending library. I learned to love to read.

"I don't remember that my mom closed the store to come to our school plays, but I remember that she was instrumental in influencing the school district to get some very good teachers in our school and to organize people to get music teachers to come from neighboring towns.

"Mom wasn't one who went with us on camping trips; it wasn't her style. But she was the one who promoted the Glenwood band, and from our little town we had a band that played in very prestigious parades, like the Calgary Stampede. She brought dignity and importance as a leader in a little town. She wasn't the traditional kind of mom, but she was the best kind of mom for me. From her I learned loyalty, dependability, industry, and endurance."

June and Ardeth looked very much alike and even sounded

alike. "If there was ever anything that was hard for us during my teenage years," Ardeth recalls, "it was that we didn't get along as I thought all mothers and daughters did. We went to mothers-and-daughters conferences, and I would sit there thinking that every other mother and daughter were getting along wonderfully except us. Then I learned later that it was not unusual for mothers and daughters to have differences during the teenage years."

Ardeth grew up surrounded by grandparents, aunts, uncles, and cousins. Her grandmother Leavitt lived across the street, and her grandmother Greene lived with Ardeth's family. The latter was an especially significant influence on Ardeth, who recalled "seeing her through the door acrack, kneeling by her bed praying. Every time she went to the temple, as I recall, she washed and ironed her temple clothes. She was always reading her scriptures and singing the hymns and smelled like lilac perfume."

The young people in Glenwood created their own entertainment, which included horseback riding, camping, holding dances, and putting on three-act plays. According to Ardeth, "When we were on stage, we thought we were the best performers they had — and we were, because we were *all* they had! And, of course, half the audience was family! Even so, it was fun to hear the applause."[2]

Because of frequent sickness, Ardeth struggled academically in school. As an incentive for her to do well, her father, who was then serving as a bishop, promised her that for her twelfth birthday he would take her with him to general conference in Salt Lake City. "Going to Salt Lake City seemed like going to the end of the world!" she exclaims. "I remember going to that conference and sitting up in the balcony on the north side and seeing the General Authorities and realizing that they were real people."[3]

Some Lessons Learned

Ardeth and her father were very close and understood each other. They spent a lot of time together on the farm, where Ardeth learned of his love for the soil and his deep reverence for life and for planting and harvesting. "Every moment with him was a teaching moment," she says. "Most of the valuable lessons, and unquestionably the lessons that gave me the greatest confidence, were outside of the classroom."

Whenever Ted had a certain look on his face, Ardeth knew he was going to teach her a lesson. One morning he said he would teach her how to jump the irrigation ditch. He put his shovel in the middle of the ditch touse as like a vaulting pole and jumped back and forth across the ditch, then handed her the shovel. Ardeth was apprehensive about the endeavor and asked, "'Dad, what if I don't make it?"

He explained, "Then you'll be in the middle."

"And if I am?"

"You'll still have to get to the other side. If you keep your eye on the other side and give it all you've got, then you'll make it."

Later that day at lunch, Ted quizzed Ardeth on what she had learned. When she replied that she had learned to jump the ditch, he said, "There will be a lot of ditches to jump in your life, and many that you'll have to jump alone. If you give it all you've got and keep your eye on the other side, you'll make it."

Helping her father build a fence taught Ardeth to keep her eye on the horizon so she would not get "discouraged by looking just at the here and now."[4] He taught that the ringing of the school bell should remind her of her inner bell, her conscience, and that she should always try to be where she was supposed to be.

During the cold Canadian winters, Ardeth got up in the mornings at the same time her father did, in order to kindle the fire. "We would stand there freezing until we got it going," she recalled. "Dad used to tell me that that chore was like faith — you have to put the wood in first to get the heat, because if you stand around to get the heat before you put in the wood, you'll never get warm."[5]

Her father was, according to Ardeth, "very, very strong on obedience and felt that it was the most important principle. He never questioned any instruction or guidance that was given by Church leaders. He obeyed any directive they gave, and he instilled that desire to obey in his family. I remember Dad as being a strong disciplinarian, but he always tempered his discipline with love and concern. Once when he spanked me, he cried. But he felt that he had to execute the discipline in order to teach me obedience. I remember thinking then that it hurt him worse than it hurt me."[6]

One evening while attending a Sunday School party, Ardeth looked at her watch and realized that she was supposed to be home. When she heard a knock at the door, she knew who it was—her father. "I was horrified," she said; "my dad had come after me. I felt humiliated in front of my friends. I thought I wanted to die. I was not pleasant with my dad; disobedience never makes one pleasant."

A few years later, she was grateful when her father came for her after a dance. She and several of her friends were driving home in a blizzard when their car stalled. Wind chill lowered the temperature to forty degrees below zero. As they soberly contemplated their plight, one friend asked Ardeth, "How long do you think it will be before your dad will get here?" It wasn't long. "This time," she said, "I was pleasant with my dad—pleasant and very grateful."[7]

Love and Marriage

One evening when Ardeth was in high school, her father asked her to stay home from a dance to fix dinner for the missionaries because her mother was in the hospital. Ardeth really wanted to go to the dance, but she was obedient to her father and prepared the meal. Elder Heber Kapp was one of the missionaries who ate dinner that evening with the Greene family. "There was something about his countenance that made me feel he was just good," Ardeth recalled. "And I had a yearning to be the kind of person someone like him would want to be with. He inspired me to be my best self."[8]

During the next year, Ardeth and Elder Kapp exchanged a few letters. However, they did not get well acquainted until after Heber completed his mission and they were each living in Provo, Utah.

During her junior year in high school, Ardeth had a mastoid

operation and missed a lot of school. Since many classes in the small Glenwood High School were only taught alternate years, she would have to wait another year to take those classes and would not be able to finish high school with her classmates. So, with her parents' permission, she went to Provo, Utah, and lived in a basement apartment with five college girls while she completed her senior year at Brigham Young High School.

"I remember feeling in my heart that my parents were giving me one more chance to do well in school, and so I felt like I just couldn't let them down," she says. "I came to school with some great uncertainties, and I probably prayed harder than I ever had before. Having prayed and done what I should, at the end of the school year I was elected representative girl of the high school. For me in that setting at that age, I felt that it was a direct answer to prayer. I felt that the Lord had heard my prayers and understood my desire to do right and just made it possible. For me it wasn't a matter of popularity; it was an answer to prayer. I really studied and did my best. I studied every available minute in the library and was one of the valedictorians after having struggled through school. I felt in my heart that in answer to my prayers, the Lord unlocked my mind."

That year, in March 1949, Heber Kapp, the missionary who had come to dinner at the Greene home in Glenwood, completed his mission, returned to his home in Ogden, Utah, and then enrolled at Brigham Young University. In Provo he looked up Ardeth, and they started dating. Of their courtship, Heber said that he was impressed by her "radiant happiness and her optimism in spite of what the situation might be. She could always see the good."[9] Ardeth and Heber became engaged the summer after Ardeth graduated from Brigham Young High. She attended BYU for one quarter and then, because her mother was not well, went home to help with the store and the family. The couple were married the following summer, on June 28, 1950, in the Alberta Temple.

Heber's mother was a widow with nine children and very little money. Heber and his brother served their missions at the same time, supported by their mother's faith and the generosity of relatives and ward members. She died of tuberculosis shortly before Ardeth and Heber were married. To help them get started

in their marriage, they borrowed some money from his grandfather. One of their first obligations as newlyweds was helping
to pay his mother's hospital and funeral expenses.

Getting an education was important to both Heber and
Ardeth. Heber planned to pursue a teaching career, so he en-
rolled for classes at Weber College, a two-year institution in
Ogden. Ardeth took a cosmetology course at Weber, thinking
that the training would enable her to help support them while
Heber completed his education. However, she went to work
instead at a clothing store, then at the telephone company in
Ogden. When Heber transferred to the University of Utah in
Salt Lake City, Ardeth transferred to the Salt Lake telephone
office.

The couple bought their first home in Kearns, a suburb
southwest of the city. Ardeth was immediately called to be the
ward YWMIA president, and Heber, the activity counselor in the
stake YMMIA. They also taught the parent and youth class — "the
only ones that didn't have a family," Ardeth says, "but they
listened to us and thought we knew. Going to a movie and eating
out would cut into people's budgets too much. We had dances
every week and everybody came. We'd go to each other's homes
after and visit and nobody had any furniture. The activity of the
Mutual was our whole social life."

After Heber graduated from the University of Utah, the
Kapps decided to go to southern California, where teachers'
wages were higher. There Heber taught school and Ardeth
worked at a phone company. When they attended their new
ward in Lakewood for the first time, the bishop introduced
himself and said, "You look like Mutual people." They were
both given callings in the MIA, and within a few weeks, Ardeth
was called as ward YWMIA president.

A year later, the Kapps returned to Utah and rented an
apartment in Bountiful, a few miles north of Salt Lake City. Before
their boxes were unpacked, the bishop of the Bountiful Third
Ward visited them and called Ardeth to be president of the
YWMIA. Heber found a teaching job, and Ardeth returned to
work at the telephone company in Salt Lake City. When she and
several co-workers noticed that some people in their office were
depressed or unhappy, they formed the Sunshine Club and

cheered up the whole office by leaving notes and complimenting and building up their associates.[10]

Building Strong Foundations

It was during this period that Heber and Ardeth began building the first of the seven homes they would eventually build in Bountiful. Novices as builders, they learned as they went by finding a home under construction and observing how certain stages of building, such as plumbing, wiring, or sheetrocking, were done. Ardeth said, "The excitement of building a home is more than just a house to live in. It is envisioning something in your mind; it's creating it on paper and negotiating with each other about what you like and what you don't like. With that visualization, then you begin to make it become a reality. There is a spirit about a home when you experience the process and seek answers on how to build it. It's a wonderful, wonderful bonding experience together because it's an accomplishment. With the Lord's help we did it.

"We are both strong individuals with strong personalities, but we resolved that if it came to a decision when we had a difference of opinion, Heber would have sway on the outside of the house and I would have sway on the inside. We both got what we wanted. It always seemed that as we looked at our budget, vast amounts of money went into concrete and wiring, and then when the house was all built, I didn't have all the money I would like for furnishings. But in the process I learned that you have to build a strong foundation, and you have to pay the price to make it sound and make it stable. You can add the extras later, but if you don't have a strong foundation, you don't have anything. There were a lot of analogies in the building process."

For years, Heber and Ardeth had dreamed of building on a lot they had purchased in Centerville, a small community north of Bountiful. They had even drawn plans for their home and built a small model of it. Then Heber was called to serve on the stake high council by Elder Spencer W. Kimball of the Quorum of the Twelve Apostles. When he told Elder Kimball that he and Ardeth planned to begin building on their lot in Centerville soon, Elder Kimball responded, "Accept the call, and everything will work out."

A month later the Kapps were ready to start building their home in Centerville. Heber recalled that when he broke the news to his stake president, "the stake president looked at me and said, 'I didn't call you to the high council. You'd better talk to the Lord.'" After discussion and prayer, Heber and Ardeth decided to sell the lot.[11]

"When we sold the lot, we thought we were saying good-bye to our dream," Ardeth remembered. "Land within our stake boundaries was too expensive. But within weeks we heard of some property in our stake that we could buy for a similar price. We bought the lot and soon had our home finished. The whole experience reminded me that we receive no witness until after the trial of our faith."[12]

Ardeth worked for the phone company for ten years, advancing from a service representative to training instructor and business office supervisor. At the time, women were not given top-level management positions, and she realized she would not have any more significant promotions. At the same time, she was also trying to understand her role in life, since it did not appear that she would become a mother. In March 1961 she returned to Glenwood for her aunt's funeral, and as she stood at the gravesite on a bitterly cold, windy day, she thought of how fleeting life is and how little time there is to make a difference. She felt impressed to return to school.

That spring Ardeth enrolled at the University of Utah. Though she was working full-time, serving in the YWMIA, and helping Heber build another house, she completed the requirements for a degree in elementary education in three years and graduated cum laude in 1964. She began teaching at a school near her home in Bountiful. The following year the dean of the College of Education at BYU asked her to supervise student teachers, an unusual assignment for a second-year teacher. The next year she wrote and produced two instructional television series, but she preferred working with students directly and returned to the classroom. In 1970, when BYU offered her a full-time faculty position supervising student teachers, she returned to the campus to work and to complete the requirements for a master's degree in curriculum development. That subject would prove particularly helpful when she was later called to serve with the Church's correlation committee and the Young Women.

"A Quarter of a Million Prayers"

When Ardeth was growing up, she dreamed of living in a small white house with a picket fence and having lots of children. She and Heber greatly desired children, prayed for them, sought the best medical expertise as well as spiritual counsel, yet were not able to have children. For months, then years, they wrestled with this disappointment.

Ardeth said, "I will forever remember the day a child new to our neighborhood knocked on our door and asked if our children could come out to play. I explained to him, as to others young and old, for the thousandth time, that we didn't have any children. This little boy squinted his innocent face in a quizzical look and asked the question that I had not dared put into words, 'If you are not a mother, then what are you?' "[13]

When Heber was called to be bishop, Ardeth realized that their childlessness was not because of unrighteousness. She related how she found peace after the trial of her faith:

"We were alone with each other at a motel in St. George, Utah, one Thanksgiving time when all our relatives were with their families. Early in the morning, I lay in bed thinking. I remember my heart crying out as I anticipated Christmas approaching. And although we could share in the joy and excitement of our nieces and nephews, it wasn't like having our own children with stockings to hang. The whole thing seemed to me to be unfair. I felt a darkness and a despondency settle over me, and I did what I'd learned to do over the years. I got on my knees and prayed for insight.

"My answer came when I opened the scriptures to Doctrine and Covenants 88:67–68: 'And if your eye be single to my glory [and remember, God's glory is to help 'to bring to pass the immortality and eternal life of man' (Moses 1:39)], your whole bodies shall be filled with light, and there shall be no darkness in you; and that body which is filled with light comprehendeth all things. Therefore, sanctify yourselves that your minds become single to God, and the days will come that you shall see him; for he will unveil his face unto you, and it shall be in his own time, and in his own way, and according to his own will.'

"I don't know how long it will be for others who have similar longings. For us it was years. But one day we did gain an eternal perspective, and we felt peace, not pain; hope, not despair. I would have liked so much to have received that insight years before, but I know that had that happened, I would have been deprived of the growth that comes from being comforted by the witness of the Spirit after the trial of my faith."[14]

One statement Heber made became "like a beacon in the dark" to Ardeth. "Speaking I think by inspiration from the Lord," she said, "the patriarch of our family said to me, 'You need not possess children to love them. Loving is not synonymous with possessing, and possessing is not necessarily loving. The world is filled with people to be loved, guided, taught, lifted, and inspired.' "[15]

Over the years, Ardeth has nurtured, guided, loved, and taught many people. When her sisters, Sharon and Shirley, were attending Brigham Young University, they would look to Heber and Ardeth for a boost whenever they needed one, according to Shirley. "As an adult, when I occasionally have those doldrum times, I give Ardie a phone call, and it's enough to pick me up to push on."[16]

Sharon lived with the Kapps for three years after she graduated from college. When Sharon's car broke down one afternoon, Ardeth loaned her her own car, asking that she bring it back by four because she had an appointment. Sharon forgot and didn't return until six o'clock. When she walked in the house, she found a cake on the table with a note that said, "I know you must have been having a wonderful time. I love you."[17]

Today Sharon's family lives near the Kapps, and her two children, Shelly and Kent, have been particularly close to their aunt. "My little brother and I call the Kapps 'Mama Ardie' and 'Papa Heber,' " Shelly said. "It's been wonderful to have another mom to go and talk to, another wonderful person to turn to. What an example of dedicating your life to the Lord! She has sacrificed her life — everything she does is in service to the Lord.

It helps me put in perspective some of the desires and wants that I have."[18]

Neighborhood children have enjoyed the cookie drawer in Ardeth's kitchen, while teenagers have often stopped by to chat or to discuss problems with the Kapps. As a ward and stake Young Women leader, Ardeth focused her attention on individual girls who she felt needed her. After she was called to serve as general president of the Young Women, she commented, "And now, after a quarter of a million prayers for children, I have responsibility for a nearly a quarter million young women. I never expected such results."[19]

Ardeth has always enjoyed expressing herself in her journals and wondered if she could write for publication. Heber encouraged her by purchasing a roll-top desk and writing materials. "I'll provide the materials," he told her, "and I'll help you provide the time. I'll do the things that take your time." He also made a wager as to whether she could get a book written before he could build the next house. She won the wager. Her first book, *Miracles in Pinafores and Blue Jeans,* was published in 1977 and became an LDS bestseller.

Since then she has published several other books, including *The Gentle Touch, All Kinds of Mothers, Echoes from My Prairie, More Miracles in Pinafores and Blue Jeans, The Light and the Life* (with Judith S. Smith), *I Walk by Faith, The Rising Generation, My Neighbor, My Sister, My Friend,* and *The Joy of the Journey.* She received Deseret Book's Excellence in Writing award in 1991. She has also published numerous articles in Church periodicals.

"Sometimes when I sit down to write I can hardly wait to get it out to see what it is that I have written," she commented. "Louisa Lula Greene Richards, the first editor of the *Woman's Exponent*, was my great-aunt. Sometimes when I'm writing I wonder if I inherited anything from her. My father was an incredible writer. He never published anything, but his journals are just like reading Mark Twain. He was so colorful and so vivid. My sisters write well, and my brother writes well. I think we lived in an environment where feelings were deep; we had a sensitivity to feelings."

Preparation for the Presidency

After serving as YWMIA president in three different wards, Ardeth had the opportunity to be a Mia Maid and a Laurel leader in her Bountiful ward. She related well to the young women, and they responded with nearly one hundred percent participation. When a few complained that because of homework and part-time jobs, they didn't have time for MIA activities, Ardeth told them she was in school also, worked full-time, and still made time for her MIA responsibilities.

In 1967 Ardeth was called to serve on the Church's youth correlation committee. When she reviewed lesson materials for young women, she concluded that they needed to be taught "matters of eternal consequence" at an earlier age, they needed Sunday instruction, their lessons should be uniquely LDS, and the scope and sequence of the curriculum needed to be evaluated. Her assignment was changed in 1971 to the newly organized curriculum development committee, where her graduate work in curriculum development was especially beneficial.

One day in October 1972, Heber and Ardeth were in the process of building another home when President Harold B. Lee's secretary called and asked if they could meet with President Lee the next morning. After a sleepless night, they met with him in his office, and he extended a call to Ardeth to serve as second counselor to Ruth Hardy Funk, the seventh general president of Young Women. Hortense H. Child was called as the first counselor.

On the Monday before Thanksgiving, Heber and Ardeth moved into their new home, and two days later Ardeth left for England on a three-week assignment. The announcement of the change of presidency had not yet reached England, and when she stepped off the plane, she could sense the disappointment of the Young Women leaders. "Isn't Sister [Florence] Jacobsen coming?" they asked. Ardeth's sense of humor helped overcome the difficult moment, for she responded, "If you feel bad about it, how do you think *I* feel?" The women all laughed and welcomed Ardeth warmly.

During the six years Ardeth served in the general presidency, many major organizational changes took place, the name of the organization was changed, and the offices were housed in three different locations. The emphasis of the presidency was to give young people more opportunities to develop leadership skills.

As second counselor, Ardeth was executive representative to the Beehive committee and to the sports and camp programs. Her background in curriculum development was again beneficial as she helped evaluate the curriculum for young women. By 1977, new, scripturally oriented manuals for the Beehive, Mia Maid, and Laurel classes were introduced. She also helped to oversee the production of *The Activity Book*, a joint undertaking of the Young Women and Young Men.

At the time Ardeth was called to serve in the general presidency, her parents, Ted and June Greene, were serving on a mission in England, where June fell and broke her hip and shoulder. When they returned, they moved into a basement apartment that Heber had built especially for them in the Kapps' new home. In February 1978, Ted Greene, who had been very active until then, doing seventy-five push-ups on his seventy-fifth birthday, was diagnosed with cancer. Ardeth was torn between needing to be at home with her parents and needing to be at the Young Women's office. Adding to this dilemma, she also received the impression that Heber would be called to be stake president.

In May, while she and Heber were vacationing in Arizona and contemplating their future, Ardeth called the office and learned that Ruth Funk wanted to see her just as soon as she returned. When they met on Mother's Day, Ruth informed her they were to be released. Ardeth returned home and told her father she would be given an honorable release. "That's all you could ask for," he responded, with tears in his eyes. "That's all I ask for, an honorable release." A week later, Heber was called as president of their stake, and five months later, on October 20, 1978, her father passed away. Her mother died on October 10, 1981.

In July 1978, immediately after her release from the Young Women presidency was announced, Ardeth received a call as Laurel adviser in her ward, which she described as "just a glorious experience." She subsequently served on the Church's instructional development writing committee. She also became a popular speaker at BYU education weeks, at "Know Your Religion" lecture programs, and at numerous stake and ward events. But the assignment she said she enjoyed most was supporting her husband as stake president.

A Woman of Vision

President Gordon B. Hinckley extended a call to Ardeth to serve as Young Women general president on April 6, 1984, the day before general conference. "He told me," said Ardeth, "that this was a very significant time, for this was a time when we were seeing great things happen in the lives of young women and that they would rise up and be a mighty force for righteousness."

Her counselors and general board were not called until several months later. During that period, Ardeth obtained a new set of scriptures and read the scriptures with young women in mind.

"That was a very crucial and valuable time for me," she remembered. "It was a time when I, in a sense, went to the mountain. I remember keeping a separate journal, which I called the small plates, of any insight or inspiration that I thought was relevant to the calling. When you have an assignment like that, there are a thousand things that you would like to ask for. You would like to ask for wisdom, people skills, righteousness. You want to be all that you should be, and you are painfully aware of the things that you are not. Sometimes I thought, 'Oh, I wish I could remember this; I wish I could remember that.' Then a thought came to me one time as I was pondering: 'I know that my Redeemer lives.' I thought, if I can know that and know that I can receive his direction, then I can look to other people for the other things I don't know. I felt that if I could have one gift during the time I would serve, the one I would most desire would be vision. If I could have a vision of what we were to accomplish and how to do it, then others with skills and ability could make it happen. But a president needs to have the vision."

Ardeth selected as her counselors Patricia Terry Holland and Maurine Johnson Turley. When Sister Holland was released in 1986, Jayne Broadbent Malan was called as a counselor. Elaine Low Jack became a counselor in 1987, replacing Sister Turley. In March 1990, Sister Jack was sustained as the Relief Society general president, and Janette Callister Hales replaced her as a counselor in Young Women.

Having gained a vision of where she should lead the young women of the Church, Ardeth worked faithfully and tirelessly to carry it out. After the presidency and board were organized, they discussed the needs of young women in the 1980s and addressed the questions of identity, direction, and purpose. "We went through a rather lengthy and soul-searching process, seeking to know what would be best for young women today," Ardeth said. "From that process, the Young Women Values — faith, divine nature, individual worth, knowledge, choice and accountability, good works, and integrity — were developed. The vision we had was that every young woman should be prepared to make and keep sacred covenants and to receive the ordinances of the temple.

"We determined that we would start with the first ordinance, baptism, so the first part of the Young Women theme is a statement of our baptismal covenant: 'We will stand as witnesses of God at all times, in all things, and in all places.' That's the foundation. It wasn't until later that we recognized there was a direct correlation between proclaiming the gospel, which is to stand as a witness for Christ; perfecting the saints, which is to live by the Young Women Values; and redeeming the dead, which is to prepare for temple ordinances. This is a foundation, just like building a house. If you don't have the foundation in place, then young women are under the pressure and storms of our day. I think that preparation for our young women today is as crucial as or more crucial than the preparation of the young pioneers who came across the plains. The tests are different. In many ways, they are more severe, more intense."

The values were introduced during the 1985 Young Women satellite broadcast, which Ardeth describes as "a landmark, historic event." The general board also produced and published a new personal progress book for the young women; introduced a mission statement and symbol for each of the three age-groups; and developed a new logo, a torch with the motto

"Stand for truth and righteousness," representing the light of Christ and inviting all young women to be bearers of the torch by keeping the commandments.

In 1987, for the first worldwide celebration of the Young Women, each young woman throughout the world was invited to write her testimony on a piece of paper, attach it to a balloon, and launch her balloon at a special program in her area. "What we wanted to have happen was to establish a worldwide sisterhood," Ardeth said. "That happened. It was an incredible thing, with young women all over the world a part of it, sending their testimonies to the world. The second worldwide celebration, the bell ringing in 1989, was a renewal of history. But more than that, it was setting in place a symbol of the ringing of the bell, which was related to listening to the Spirit and a recommitment to follow the prophet."

Ardeth subscribes to the proverb "Where there is no vision, the people perish." (Proverbs 29:18.) She believes that leaders must give people a vision of who they are and why they do what they do, and she conveys that vision through her own leadership style and through training others to be leaders. She also believes that individuals cannot do the work of the Lord unless they continually study the word of the Lord. Thus, members of her board devoted thirty to forty-five minutes of their weekly board meetings to studying the scriptures.

Obedient to the direction of the Brethren, Ardeth believes in priesthood power and authority and teaches that there is only one organizational channel, the priesthood channel. Maurine Turley said, "She taught her counselors and board members the importance of the priesthood line and that we are a resource to the priesthood leadership. She always taught Young Women leaders to honor their priesthood leaders and to follow their direction."[20]

Ardeth's leadership style, according to Patricia Holland, enables others to grow. "No one is better than Ardeth in developing leadership because she is so wonderful in giving encouragement and praise. She delegated significant responsibilities to her counselors, and we were accountable for them. She just let go and trusted us."[21] When Elaine Jack was called to serve as the Relief Society general president in March 1990, she paid tribute to Ardeth, declaring, "She has tutored me, encouraged me, and allowed me to grow."[22]

Ardeth has always found time for people. Carolyn J. Rasmus, her administrative assistant, recalled that once after a BYU football game, when Ardeth was in a hurry to get to another event, "People seeing her called out, 'Sister Kapp, Sister Kapp,' and she stopped to talk with them as if she had all the time in the world. I have never seen her annoyed or impatient. Over and over again I have seen her be nothing but generous and lifting and building to people."[23]

Ardeth carried on what she termed "a ministry by mail" with young women who wrote to her, responding to every letter written to her by thousands of them. She also ministered one-on-one. Janette Hales observed that Ardeth often asked local leaders to identify a young woman who had a special need and then went with the local leader and often a youth leader to visit that individual. "I think that was one of the most tender and gentle things she did. She inspired people with problems to see their potential," Janette said. "In some cases, I don't think they knew who she was, but they felt her spirit. Sister Kapp always asked if she could pray with the young woman in her home, then bore a strong testimony of the girl's divine potential. She described it as 'being on the Lord's errand.' "[24]

Through training seminars and the *Young Women Leadership Guidebook* (1990) and *Young Women Leadership Video* (1991), Ardeth trained many leaders and many young women themselves. "One thing I hope our administration will be remembered for," she said, "was changing the mindset from saying 'What shall we do?' to the question 'What do we want to have happen?' — so that we're not focusing on activities but looking at outcomes."

Ardeth has a keen sense of humor and an ability to laugh. Patricia Holland said, "I'm never around her more than five minutes before she has me laughing. She's either just had a funny experience or has a funny story to tell. She's willing at her own expense to be funny. That's one of the things that endears her to you."[25]

Jayne Malan noted, "We really have fun in social situations. But even in social situations Ardeth is always looking at the principle of why are we doing this — is it to develop sisterhood or to build team unity? She has a marvelous sense of humor and a good sense of timing. In fact, I think her sense of timing goes right along with her leadership — she is so visionary."[26]

Heber totally supported Ardeth in her calling, helping with grocery shopping, household chores, and cooking. She was sometimes concerned about the amount of time she was away from home, but he urged her to do every possible assignment, saying, "You won't have this calling forever, and when the time comes to be released, you won't have one regret if you have given it all you have. Don't hold back; just give every ounce of energy, and when you are released you'll know you've done the best you could."

Ardeth has received many honors, including the Lambda Delta Sigma Elect Lady Award (1986); Collegium Aesculapium Humanitarian Award from the Brigham Young Academy of Medicine (1989); Utah-California Women Heritage Award (1990); and Exemplary Womanhood Award from the BYU Student Association (1990). Her community involvement has included serving on the Bountiful City Citizens Planning Commission for development of library and educational services and on a University of Utah Graduate School advisory council subcommittee to develop a high school curriculum on parenting. She has also served on the Board of Trustees for the Church Educational System, on boards of directors for Deseret Gymnasium and Deseret Book Company, and as a member of the National Coalition Against Pornography.

A New Mission to Serve

On January 3, 1992, Heber received a call to serve as a mission president. Ardeth was released as general president of the Young Women at general conference on April 4, and in July they began presiding over the Canada Vancouver Mission. There she continues to bless lives and to provide vision.

Ardeth Greene Kapp learned the lesson of obedience early in her life — obedience to her parents, obedience to the priesthood, obedience to the Spirit, and obedience to the Lord. She

overcame unfulfilled expectations and turned her heart to nurturing and serving others. Throughout her life and throughout
her service as the general president of the Young Women, she
sought to know the Lord's will and to carry it out. She is indeed
a woman of vision.

10

Janette Callister Hales

1992–

When Janette Callister Hales was a young girl, she loved to go to the carnival that periodically stopped in her hometown of Spanish Fork, Utah. The pink cotton candy, cold root beer, ferris wheel, merry-go-round, and games of skill were a dazzling array of attractions for young Janette — and she was always eager for one more ride or one more treat.

One year when the carnival was in town for the Twenty-fourth of July, Janette's father handed her a silver dollar and said, "Here, go enjoy yourself and buy whatever you want." When carnival items cost a nickel or a dime, a silver dollar represented a small fortune to an eight-year-old.

"I remember going with my girlfriends to the carnival," Janette said. "I priced everything — cotton candy, the rides — and I figured out how many of each thing I could get for my dollar. At the end of the day, I came home with my dollar. I hadn't spent any of it. I realized that it was my dollar, and all of a sudden that had more value because it represented choice. By keeping the dollar, I still had the choice. Once it was gone, the choice was gone."

Throughout her life, Janette has always placed a high value on her right, as well as the rights of others, to choose. This valuing of choice has shaped her relationships with people: she facilitates growth in others through her nurturing attitude, her wise counsel, and her ability to help people realize the consequences of their choices.

Strong Family Ties

Janette was born June 7, 1933, in Springville, Utah, to Thomas Leonard and Hannah Carrick Callister. The third child in the family—she has two older sisters, Colleen and Marilyn—she was named Janette after her paternal grandmother, Janetta. Three other children were born into the family: Geraldine, Thomas John (who died at age five), and EnaMarie (who died in infancy). The family lived in Spanish Fork, a small farming community ten miles south of Provo.

Thomas's parents, Thomas and Janetta Crellin Callister, had emigrated to the United States from the Isle of Man in the 1890s. The lure of the new country and opportunities for farming and mining brought them west to Santaquin, Utah, twenty-two miles south of Provo. Janetta, a staunch Presbyterian, attended church, even though she had to travel to Provo to find a congregation. When their son Thomas was eighteen, the Callisters moved to Provo. Neither he nor his parents joined The Church of Jesus Christ of Latter-day Saints.

Janette's maternal grandmother, Ena Gudmundson, joined the Church as a young girl, along with her family in Vestmannaeyjar, Iceland. Since there wasn't enough money to allow the whole family to immigrate to Utah together at that time, Ena stayed behind and came with another family in 1886, when she was twelve. After arriving in Utah, she worked in a shoe factory and did housework. Janette's grandfather, John James Carrick, came to the United States from England in 1888. He and Ena were married in 1895. His work as a miner took them to Hiawatha, a small town in eastern Utah. They then moved to Canada for about a year to find work during a mining slump. There Janette's mother, Hannah, was born.

When John and Ena Carrick returned to Utah, Ena felt that a mining community wasn't a healthy environment for children, so the family purchased a small farm in Mapleton, eight miles south of Provo. John worked in the mines during the week and came home on weekends. Ena raised raspberries and milked cows and also became a practical nurse.

Janette, who still feels "strong ties to her Icelandic heritage," was greatly influenced by her grandmother Carrick. "I felt that my grandmother could do anything, although she never learned to read and write in English. As a practical nurse, she would stay with women when they had their babies. She would be there to assist with the delivery and then stay ten days and care for the newborn and the mother and cook for the family. For years, even when I was in college, I regularly met people who said my grandmother had taken care of them.

"One memorable thing about my grandmother was her hearty laugh. I remember how secure I would feel when I could hear her laughing. I was about eight years old when my grandfather died, and so my grandmother became even more a part of all our family occasions. When there were babies born in our family or extra hands were needed, Grandma was always there. I slept with her when she stayed with us, and periodically I would spend a few days in her home. She always had her hands busy. She taught me to crochet. Since she was left-handed, I would watch what she would do, then I would have to move away and reverse her instructions in my mind because I was right-handed."

Janette grew up in a secure and loving home with parents who made her feel that she could do whatever she wanted to do. "My father was such a good man," said Janette, "and so respected by others for his integrity. I guess I idolized my dad. He sang and always whistled a tune as he came up the walk and into the house. He was witty and loved to tease as well as to stimulate a good debate."

An experience that profoundly affected Janette and her family began one day when she was in the third grade. "I remember Grandma Carrick being there to get us off to school," she recalled. "It was unusual for my mother not to be in the kitchen fixing breakfast. I was told only that she was upstairs. Grandma hurried us out the door much earlier than usual. Later that morning, my father came running out on to the playground at my elementary school with a smile from ear to ear and announced that I had a new baby brother. I don't remember ever seeing my parents happier. My father had no brothers and had longed for a son and someone to carry on his family name. The baby was named Thomas John Callister after his two grandfathers. Although Tommy was born jaundiced, it was many weeks before my parents realized that he was not developing as a normal child. His rigid responses and inability to reach for a toy led my family to realize only years later that he had a type of cerebral palsy. Medical science at that time never made a clear diagnosis. Tommy was subject to infections and died at the age of five.

"It was during this period that I learned the most about a mother's unconditional love. Although my parents sought in vain for medical answers that would improve his condition, I watched my mother work tirelessly to provide warmth, food, and happiness to a child who never learned to sit, feed himself, or even be able to pick up a toy. This was a setting in which I learned much about sensitivity, caring, and compassion. These were war years and a time of stress for most families, but it was a period when I saw motherhood nobly modeled. My parents sold two building lots adjacent to our home, which my mother had always gardened, in order to have money to bury two children."

Though her father was not a member of the Church and her mother did not attend church at that time, Janette occasionally went to Primary with her friends. "I was passing off the Articles of Faith at the home of the Primary president," she recounted. "After I finished, she took my hand and asked me, 'Wouldn't you like to be baptized?' "[1] She was baptized shortly before her eleventh birthday, on the same day as her sister Geri, who was eight. Her parents supported her decision, Janette said. "They'd always taught gospel principles in our home. . . . They taught me to be kind, honest, and loving, and they supported me in everything I ever did."[2] With her parents' encouragement, Janette attended church meetings on Sundays with her friends. Her father frequently chauffeured her and her friends to various church functions.

Caring leaders also played a great role in Janette's life. "I remember being influenced positively by caring adults," she said. "Part of that was being in a small community; part was the Church as well. There were always people extending themselves for me. I always had parts in plays and in things that were happening at church. Throughout my school years I participated in student government and in many other activities."

When Janette reached high school, her MIA attendance was sporadic, since she worked in the evenings at the local movie theater. After she graduated from high school, she worked during the day and was called as the YWMIA secretary. She developed a close relationship with the other leaders and advisers.

Following her father's advice that she should learn "how to do something," Janette learned accounting, shorthand, and typing. But she also felt she wanted something more. She looked to the example of her sister Colleen, who was the first member of their extended family to graduate from college.

A Turning Point

Janette, an outstanding student in high school, received a scholarship to Brigham Young University—twenty-five dollars for tuition for one quarter. It was, she said, a "bleak time" for her when she turned the scholarship over to the alternate because she did not have enough money to pay for her other expenses. "I was only eighteen, yet I thought my life was over," she said. When her friends went off to college, she worked for a family doctor in Spanish Fork at a twelve-bed hospital and learned many new skills. She recalled doing "everything from developing X-rays to blood tests to filling out birth certificates and giving bed baths as well as doing the billing and accounting for the doctor's practice and the hospital."

The next fall Janette enrolled at BYU and thought she would be very fortunate if her savings carried her through the year. Housing was scarce in Provo, but she managed to find a room over a garage to share with a high school friend. After two quarters, her roommate dropped out of school and went home, but Janette had found a part-time job and renewed her commitment to stay in school. "That was a real turning point in my life," she said. "I really began to work hard academically. I was invited to join the freshman honor society and was also invited to join a social unit. I started to make new friends. I also started to feel what a mature adult life was, and an extended view of the possibilities started to come." She decided to major in clothing and textiles, partly because of the sewing expertise she learned from her mother.

During her second year of college, Janette roomed with
seven other girls in a small house off-campus. They got up each
morning at 6:30 — even though some of them didn't have classes
until ten o'clock — for family prayer and breakfast and then met
again at night for dinner. One roommate commented after the
group had missed a day or two of praying together, "Things just
don't go right when we don't have prayer." For Janette, this
became a strong family situation. "That environment was a really
good influence on me as I attended weekly devotionals and took
religion classes. I made some strong commitments in terms of
life-style and the future by the time I finished my sophomore
year."

Marriage and Motherhood

A mutual friend introduced Janette to a young man who
had recently returned from a mission in England, Robert H.
Hales. He was well known at BYU and had been selected as one
of the "Ten Most Preferred Men on Campus." Their paths crossed
occasionally and Janette admired him secretly, but it was not
until she was a sophomore and Bob was a student at the University of Utah College of Medicine that they began dating. Because of Bob's demanding studies, their dates were few and far
between. In the spring of 1955, after a year's courtship, they
became engaged. Janette admired Bob's ambition, willingness
to work hard, and natural leadership abilities. "Material things
were of little importance to him," she said, "but experience and
opportunity really were. He opened a new world of adventure
for me." She had planned to run for president of the BYU
Associated Women Students and had had her photograph taken
for her campaign. Instead, she used the picture for her engagement photo. She and Bob were married June 29, 1955, in
the Salt Lake Temple.

Janette worked as a secretary/accountant at the Wheel-
wright Lithographing Company to help her husband through
school. Ann, their first daughter, was born in 1956, as her father
entered his last year of medical school. Following graduation,
the young family moved to San Antonio, Texas, where Bob had
a medical internship at Lackland Air Force Base. They planned

on being in Texas only a year and were short on money, so they didn't buy an air conditioner — the only military family they knew that didn't have one. Janette was pregnant with their second child, Thomas, and Bob's work schedule was often intense — every day and every other night. She found herself uncomfortably hot, lonely, and frustrated. Bob would come home and say, "Why don't you just go shopping and buy you something?" Her reply was, "Where will I wear it?" She described this experience as "a real growing-up year for me. I was very naive. It was just part of my going from a childish expectation to a more mature, realistic view."

Activity in the Church helped Janette adjust to being away from her family in Utah and to her role as a military doctor's wife. She served as a counselor in both the Relief Society presidency and the YWMIA presidency in their branch. The family's stay in San Antonio extended through a second hot summer, for after Bob completed his internship, he was invited to attend the school of aviation medicine at Randolph Air Force Base.

Bob's next assignment was as a flight surgeon at Mitchell Air Force Base on Long Island, near New York City. Janette especially enjoyed this period of their lives. "That was like a paid vacation for me and was the only time in our married life that we had 'normal hours,' " she recalled. "We assumed that we would live in the West someday, so we took advantage of everything. We went to Washington, D.C., Boston, Palmyra, and New York City. Through the USO we could get free tickets to Broadway plays when they were near the end of their runs. Bob's uncle, David J. Wilson, was a judge of the Customs Court in New York, and his aunt, Mary Wilson, included me in a lot of her social activities. I had some wonderful opportunities."

The Haleses attended the Uniondale Ward, where Janette served as a Laurel leader and chorister in the MIA, and Bob taught Sunday School and served as president of the elders quorum.

After living in New York for two years, the family moved to San Francisco, where Bob began his residency in ophthalmology at the University of California Medical Center. As soon as they attended church in San Francisco's Sunset Ward, Janette was asked to be Primary president. "That period of my life changed me the most as far as spiritual growth and commitment," she said. "I think I extended myself more in church callings and leadership. I had some spiritual experiences that really changed me. If I were to relate to that 'mighty change of heart' that Alma talks about, I think it came during that period. Prior to that, I felt totally committed and that I had a testimony, but now there was a change. The gospel became more personal to me." Seeking to finish her degree in home economics, she learned that the only classes she could take by correspondence were religion classes. "I have a tremendous reverence for the scriptures that goes back to that period," she commented.

Jane, Janette and Bob's third child, was born in San Francisco in 1962. The following year, the family returned to Provo, where Bob set up a solo practice. Janette remembered this as an exciting time, in spite of the severity of that first winter, an old car that had to be jump-started every morning, and the financial uncertainty of a new medical practice. Two more daughters joined the family: Karen in 1965 and Mary in 1967. The children all helped at the office, cleaning it "almost as soon as they could walk" and later doing the billing. Working with their father helped keep the family united.

Family Traditions

When Bob was growing up, his father, Wayne B. Hales, a physics professor at BYU, taught summer school classes at Aspen Grove, a university-owned family camp in nearby Provo Canyon. Bob loved those mountains and wanted to have a cabin where the family could spend time together. Although their five children slept in two small bedrooms in the Hales home in Provo, Bob and Janette purchased a canyon lot. "I dragged my feet in buying the lot, but building a summer home became a strong source of family unity," said Janette. Bob especially liked to hike to the top of nearby Mount Timpanogos, and he would often take the children and their friends along. Janette hiked to the top only once; she preferred staying at the cabin to prepare dinner for the returning hikers. Jane Hales Ricks has happy memories of the family gathering at the cabin to listen to general conference. That tradition always included her mother fixing her "Sundance Special" breakfast: an English muffin with broiled cheese, Canadian bacon, and an egg "over lightly."[3]

Seeking knowledge has been a strong Hales family tradition. Janette used to study college catalogs just for the fun of contemplating what she would take if she had the time and means. When her youngest child, Mary, was a year old, Janette received a bachelor's degree in clothing and textiles from BYU — having finished her senior year over a period of thirteen years.

Bob's mother, Belle, had died the year the Haleses returned to Provo, so Grandfather Hales frequently ate dinner with the family, often bringing a stack of books for the children. Besides Bob's medical discussions at the dinner table, the children heard lessons about the physical world from their grandfather.

Janette was very close to her father-in-law, Wayne Hales. "He was an ideal to me in a religious sense, yet he allowed me to be myself," she said. "I would sometimes question him on things, and he would say to me, 'Janette, you ask hard questions.' I felt that he loved me totally. We had a very caring relationship. He was so appreciative of the mothering kinds of things I did — like fixing him a bowl of hot cereal. He made me feel as if I were just wonderful." During his final illness, Janette helped care for him. She had taken a class on care of the terminally ill and determined that no matter what it took on her part, she wanted to do all she could to make it a "good occasion" for him. They became even closer during this experience. He died in 1980.

"Dad Hales was a great influence on the children. His desire for learning just infused his life," said Janette. "He gave a lesson every time a cloud went overhead. My children were all good students, and I don't ever remember taking responsibility for their schoolwork. One of Ann's junior high teachers asked me one day, 'How do you get your children to study so much?' That was the time I was trying to graduate, so studying is just what we did. It was a way of life for all of us."

Ann received degrees in nursing and law; Tom has a Ph.D. in math and teaches at the University of Chicago; Jane completed medical school and works part-time at the BYU Health Center; Karen obtained a master's degree in organizational behavior, has taught Japanese and math at a private school, and is pursuing a degree in education at Columbia Teachers College; and Mary is pursuing a degree in dietetics. "My mother always had a very practical view of education," said Ann. "She saw education as a means of increasing our abilities and as a way of preparing us to help other people. She did not have an ivory tower approach of education for its own sake."[4]

Music has been another family tradition, partly because of Janette's unfulfilled desire to have music lessons when she was young. She can now play hymns on the piano, thanks to practicing done while she waited for people. "The more I waited, the better I played," she mused. "When I would get dinner ready and be waiting for Bob to come home from the office — and his hours were not always predictable — I practiced instead of getting frustrated." Ann learned to play the piano, Tom the clarinet and oboe, Jane the flute, Karen the violin, and Mary the cello. Jane sometimes resisted practicing and would ask, "How long do I have to play the flute?" Her mother would reply, "You don't have to play the flute. If you would rather vacuum two hours a day, you don't have to practice."[5]

By the time the children reached high school, Janette felt that it was their choice whether to continue with music lessons. Ann, who was quite accomplished on the piano, decided that she wanted to diversify how she spent her time, so she chose to spend less time practicing. "Mom always expressed her faith in our ability to make choices," she said, "and she always let us make our choices and learn from the consequences. I see her in a mentor role, facilitating people to grow."[6]

"Mother never tried to put us in a mold of what she thought we should be," according to Karen Hales Parkinson. "Rather, she supported us and helped us discover the realities of our quests." When Janette went shopping with Karen for patterns and fabric, she would allow Karen to select the color and design she wanted, and though Karen's choices were sometimes out-landish, her mother always found a way to make the outfit look attractive.[7] "Mom never regulated our lives, but let our best selves come out," Jane said. She also noted that her mother disciplined with hugs, not reprimands. When Jane broke her expensive new tennis racket and finally found the courage to show it to her mother, Janette responded by hugging her and saying it was all right.[8]

Janette took up tennis when she was nearly forty years old. A neighbor, the tennis coach at BYU, offered to teach tennis to the women in the neighborhood. Janette said, "We showed up for our first lesson in the worst garb you could imagine — long pants and the wrong kind of shoes, but Wayne Pearce made us believe that we could play. I particularly felt that I had some natural ability. It was just contagious for me. Then as I played people who were a little younger, a little faster, and had more experience, it began to be not so much fun. I remember going home one day and saying maybe I should be spending my time on other things. I think that's how we often justify quitting — we always have something else that's more valuable. The selection of an alternative activity wasn't the point. The point was, when it got hard I wanted to quit. My daughter Jane said, 'Why don't you wait until you get good and then decide whether to quit?' "

Janette did not quit. She has played tennis several times a week for the past twenty years, and she and Jane once played in a league together. Karol S. Gleave, Janette's tennis partner for fifteen years, commented, "Janette is aggressive and competitive on the tennis court, which makes her a lot of fun to play with. She feels that playing tennis helps to keep balance in her life."[9] "People on the tennis court know I'm very competitive," Janette agreed. "Competition at its best is a form of cooperation. If you want to grow you have to push on something. Muscles have to have something to push on to grow."

Although she and Bob worked closely together as husband and wife, Janette maintained a strong sense of her own identity apart from being a wife or mother. "I was always aware of my parents doing things together, but it was important to my mother to have her own identity from her own efforts," her daughter Mary said. "She was quite independent."[10] Janette discovered that as she did things for herself, such as playing tennis, she could allow her children to have their successes and she could have hers. "I believe that mothers make a real mistake by requiring their children to meet the mother's needs," she explained. "It's a real burden for a child."

Not only did Janette encourage her own children to grow

by helping them examine the consequences of their choices
and by providing resources to develop potential, but she has
also provided such opportunities to many others as well. Having
been raised with limited resources, she is sensitive to the needs
of others and likes to encourage people to keep working. For
many years she has maintained a checking account called the
"Janette C. Hales Special Fund." She sends small checks and
letters to encourage young people to continue developing their
talents. "There is no plan to it," she said. "I just do it when the
Spirit tells me."

Over the years she and Bob acquired a fine collection of
paintings by Utah artists. By purchasing works of some artists
who were at the time not well-known, they encouraged further
artistic development. When Dan Ricks, Jane's husband, was looking for a job the summer before he started medical school,
Janette suggested that if he wanted to wash windows, she would
set him up in business. She supplied him with a ladder, squee-
gees, cleaning supplies, and an instruction book and let him
practice on her windows. Dan did well financially, and the experience also increased his desire to go to school so he wouldn't
have to wash windows the rest of his life.

Friendships and Service

"Because my own parents didn't participate in church,
friendships have been really important to me," remarked Janette.
"Friends are like additional family. I have very close friendships,
and they seem really necessary." She maintains many friendships
developed over the years and enjoys planning reunions with
her San Antonio friends, New York friends, San Francisco friends,
and college roommates. She is close to her tennis partners,
neighbors, and ward members. According to her daughter Ann,
her "excellent people skills and her ability to help people reach
their potential" have endeared her to many people.[11]

Mary Alice Collins, Janette's next-door neighbor for over
twenty years, said, "We have a fabulous neighborhood. Five
families on our street have children about the same ages, and
so we have raised them together. The children have felt that
they could go to any of the adults for help. My youngest daughter

and her friend had missed the school bus several times, so one morning when they had missed it again, they felt hesitant to face their mothers, so they went to Janette's house and asked her to drive them to school—which she did. Janette is a wonderful cook and invited all the neighborhood children to her home one day for scones. She has provided fun games for neighborhood parties, made a video of the neighborhood, and written words for a neighborhood song."[12] Ann Edwards Cannon, who grew up in that neighborhood and was a friend of Ann Hales, stated, "Janette was genuinely friendly to her children's friends. Whenever I went to their home, I felt very invited."[13]

Janette and Bob both lived their philosophy of extending service beyond the family circle. A Hales family joke was, "Whatever Dad wasn't president of, Mom was."[14] While Bob served as a bishop and then as a counselor in the stake presidency, Janette served as president of the Utah County Medical Auxiliary, as a PTA president, and as a member of the curriculum committee of the Provo School District. In the Church, she served as gospel doctrine teacher, Young Women adviser and counselor, an instructor at the Missionary Training Center, and ward Relief Society president. The latter experience had a particularly profound effect upon her, she said. "My heart was so full of love for everyone in the ward. Women that I hadn't thought of being my best friends—I loved every one of them. I committed Thursdays to doing Relief Society visits. When I woke up each Thursday morning, names came into my head and I knew exactly where to go and what to do. It was a wonderful process."

"A Good Life Ahead"

The youngest of the Hales children, Mary, was preparing to serve a mission when Bob noticed swelling in his knee and shortness of breath. He scheduled an appointment for an examination on his day off. Janette returned home from playing tennis and found a note on the kitchen table to go to the hospital. There she learned that Bob had a malignant tumor that had spread throughout his body. "At that point, my world fell apart," she said. "Yet I felt I had some experiences that helped prepare me for Bob's death. We were able to talk through everything. He was able to be at home until just two days before he died. He handled it so courageously himself." Bob died in March 1988, just four weeks after being diagnosed with cancer.

Shortly after Bob's death, Janette put her arms around Karen and Mary, who were still at home, and told them, "I just know we have a good life ahead. I know we will be happy. I know there will be compensations." Thomas C. Hales said, "It was when my dad died that I first really saw the strengths of my mom. Until then, they were so much of a team that I never really thought to assess the strengths of my mom versus the strengths of my dad. A number of people who were grieving the loss of a spouse talked to my mother. She saw that many had stopped growing, and she was determined not to let that happen to her."[15]

Janette found herself doing a lot of walking at that time and thinking a lot about youth. One day she told a neighbor, "If I ever have a chance to work with young people again, I will be so much more patient, so much more gentle, and so much more loving. . . . I will do all in my power to encourage young people to prepare for the future."[16]

Five months after Bob's death, Janette was called to the Primary general board. Virginia H. Pearce, a fellow board member, observed that as she and Janette served on a committee to prepare training materials for stake leaders, Janette was reluctant to impose policies but rather focused on principles, adding, "She is very willing to trust other people and to let them grow. She feels that life is a process, not a product."[17]

Prior to his illness, Bob had encouraged Janette to get involved in politics. Just weeks after his death, she read in the newspaper that her state representative was moving from the area, so she filed to run for the legislature. She was appointed by Governor Norman Bangerter to fill the vacancy in the state legislature, then was elected to the Utah State House of Representatives in the November general election. "I love the process of free government," she said. "It is a problem-solving process, when people with diverse opinions and backgrounds work together. What you're really trying to do is combine needs and resources in such a way that growth can take place — economic growth or educational growth, for instance." She served for one term; in 1990, the next election year, she withdrew her name for reelection when she was called to serve in the general presidency of Young Women.

When Elaine L. Jack was released as a counselor in the Young Women general presidency in March 1990 and was sustained as the general president of the Relief Society, Janette Hales was called to serve as second counselor to Ardeth G. Kapp.

"Although I was not well acquainted with Janette at the time I requested that she be called to serve as my counselor in the Young Women general presidency, I felt drawn to her in a spiritual sense," Ardeth recalled. "I had a great desire to become acquainted with her. I felt that I could learn from her, and she had much to give. As we began working together, immediately a sense of trust was developed for her loyalty, her judgment, her sensitivity, and her wise and gentle counsel. She has the ability to weigh carefully and speak clearly. Void of pride and any selfish motives, she is free to be true to her own convictions while showing deep respect for another's point of view. Her genuine reverence for the uniqueness and value of each individual is ever apparent. In matters of principle, she stands firm. In matters of practice, she demonstrates wise judgment."[18]

Janette has an unusual ability to analyze situations and to respond wisely. "As I was growing up, my friends all thought I was so wise," her daughter Mary said. "When we talked about problems, I just repeated the answers my mother had given me when we had discussed those same issues earlier."[19]

When one of the secretaries at the Young Women office was hospitalized on Secretaries' Day, Carolyn Rasmus, administrative assistant for the Young Women president, asked Janette if she should put "Happy Secretaries' Day" on the card accompanying the flowers the office was sending. Janette responded, "We probably shouldn't impose how a person should feel in the hospital. Let's write 'It's Secretaries' Day. We're thinking of you, and we care about you.' " "That was a real lesson for me," Carolyn commented. "That is wisdom."[20]

Janette had served earlier as a counselor to Patricia Pinegar in a Relief Society presidency in their Provo ward. Patricia said, "Whenever I am in the same room with Janette Hales, I take notes—whether she's teaching a gospel doctrine lesson, giving a talk in sacrament meeting, or conducting a meeting. She has such wonderful wisdom; it is profound in its simplicity."[21]

Tenth General President of Young Women

Janette served as a counselor in the Young Women general presidency for two years; then another significant change occurred in her life. Ardeth Kapp's husband, Heber, was called in early 1992 to serve as a mission president, necessitating Ardeth's release as general president. Janette Hales was selected to succeed her.

"I had some experiences of preparation before President Thomas S. Monson extended the call to me to serve as Young Women general president," Janette recalled. "Those experiences had given me a feeling of being overwhelmed with self-doubt. One morning when I had been feeling discouraged, I was driving past Temple Square and looked over at the tabernacle and thought of all that had happened to me in the past four years. My life had changed so much. When my daughter Mary said that her bishop wanted her to be a Sunday School teacher and that she didn't feel like a teacher, I said, 'You're not yet, Mary, but you will be.' I thought, I'm not this and I'm not that, but I'm not all I'm going to be. We're not finished until we get to the end of our lives. All of a sudden I had a wonderful optimistic feeling and the cloud was gone."

Between the time she received the call and the announcement at general conference in April, she had an experience that was reaffirming to her:

"I woke up one night and thought of Enos praying. He was taking on a new responsibility as his father, Jacob, had entrusted him with the plates. [See Jacob 7:27.] His experience had real meaning as to how I felt about being able to do what I had been called to do.

" 'There came a voice unto me, saying: Enos, thy sins are forgiven thee, and thou shalt be blessed.

" 'And I, Enos, knew that God could not lie; wherefore, my guilt was swept away. And I said: Lord, how is it done?

" 'And he said unto me: Because of thy faith in Christ, whom thou hast never before heard nor seen. And many years pass away before he shall manifest himself in the flesh; wherefore, go to, thy faith hath made thee whole.

"'Now it came to pass that when I heard these words I began to feel a desire for the welfare of my brethren.' [Enos 1: 5–9.]

"I realized that faith helps us overcome our deficits whether they are sins or other feelings of inadequacy. We really become who we become because of the gift of the Atonement. And thinking of the welfare of others makes us other-oriented instead of self-oriented. What has the Savior asked us to do but to love one another and to serve one another?"

On April 4, 1992, Janette was sustained as the tenth general president of the Young Women. She chose Virginia Hinckley Pearce and Patricia Peterson Pinegar as her counselors. At the time of their calling, the new presidency had responsibility for nearly half a million young women residing in 138 nations and territories.

"Janette works in an atmosphere of peace and calmness," said Patricia Pinegar. "She says, 'We can do this. You can do this.' She allows us time to learn and to grow and to take these callings one step at a time. She gives me confidence that I can serve as her counselor."[22]

"Janette is so right for the time," according to Virginia Pearce. "Young women leaders need to do for their young women what Janette is doing for us in allowing us to grow. She gives us assignments without imposing her expectations on what the outcome should be. One feels so responsible to that trust."[23]

When the presidency met together for the first time, Janette discussed scriptures that had to do with heart. "If I had one theme, it is the great need to touch people's hearts with the spirit of the gospel," she remarked. "The last verse of Malachi states, 'He shall turn the heart of the fathers to the children, and the heart of the children to their fathers.' [Malachi 4:6.] I had always thought of that scripture in terms of family history. But now I also think about it in terms of turning the hearts of the adults to the youth and the hearts of the youth to the adults and making an environment of love." In the April 1992 general conference, in her first address as Young Women general president, she challenged, "To every adult member of the Church, may I suggest that you learn the names of the young people in your ward or branch and call them by name. Encourage them in their work efforts. Recognize them for the good things they do. They need our support, and we need theirs."[24]

Ardeth Kapp observed of her successor: "Janette speaks of and demonstrates four points she uses to give direction to her life: (1) prepare carefully, (2) communicate honestly, (3) have courage to represent whomever you have been asked to represent, and (4) be obedient. Her lifetime preparation has prepared her well for the remarkable service that she will perform in building the kingdom and blessing the lives of women, older and younger."[25]

"Because of Janette's great respect for individuals, she wants to reach out and make a difference in people's lives personally," stated Carolyn Rasmus. "For her, the real work is one on one, in the opportunity to talk heart to heart and to listen heart to heart. I believe her greatest contribution will be in the quiet ways she reaches out and touches hearts."[26]

Young Women Time Line

1820	Joseph Smith receives First Vision
1829	Restoration of the Aaronic and Melchizedek priesthoods
1830	Publication of the Book of Mormon; The Church of Jesus Christ of Latter-day Saints is organized on April 6 in Fayette, New York
1830–1844	Joseph Smith serves as first prophet and president of Church
1835	Doctrine and Covenants is published
1836	Kirtland Temple is dedicated
1842	Female Relief Society of Nauvoo is organized
1843	Young Gentlemen's and Ladies' Relief Society of Nauvoo is organized
1844	Female Relief Society is disbanded; Joseph and Hyrum Smith are martyred
1844–77	Brigham Young presides over the Church
1846	Nauvoo Temple is dedicated
1847	First pioneer wagon company enters Salt Lake Valley
1850	University of Deseret (later University of Utah) is established
1861–65	U.S. Civil War
1866	Female Relief Society is reorganized
1866–80	Eliza R. Snow leads all women's auxiliaries

1869	Brigham Young organizes the Young Ladies' Department of the Cooperative Retrenchment Association (Young Ladies' Retrenchment Association)
1869	Transcontinental railroad is completed at Promontory, Utah
1870	Women in Utah receive the right to vote
1875	Young Men's Mutual Improvement Association is organized; joint meetings are held monthly, but organizations remain separate
1877	Name is changed to Young Ladies' National Mutual Improvement Association; St. George Temple is dedicated
1877–87	John Taylor presides over the Church
1878	First YLMIA stake board is organized in Salt Lake Stake; Primary is organized
1880	Separate presidencies are called for Primary, YLMIA, and Relief Society; YLMIA central board is organized
1880–1904	ELMINA SHEPARD TAYLOR serves as first general president of Young Ladies' Mutual Improvement Association
1887	Edmunds-Tucker Act is passed, disfranchising Utah women
1887–98	Wilford Woodruff presides over the Church
1889	*Young Woman's Journal* is published, with Susa Young Gates as editor
1890	Manifesto is issued, discontinuing practice of polygamy
1891	YLMIA affiliates with National Council of Women
1893	Instructions and lessons are printed in the *Guide* (later published in *Young Woman's Journal*); Tuesday night is designated Mutual night; Salt Lake Temple is dedicated
1894	Annual Day is begun as a sports event

1896	Utah is granted statehood and women regain right to vote; YLMIA and YMMIA hold joint conference
1898	Traveling MIA libraries are begun
1898–1901	Lorenzo Snow, fifth president of Church
1900	YLMIA chorus sings in Tabernacle at June Conference
1901–18	Joseph F. Smith, sixth president of Church
1902	Joint opening exercises are held for young men and young women
1904	Name is changed to Young Ladies' Mutual Improvement Association
1905–29	MARTHA HORNE TINGEY serves as second president of YLMIA
1909	Women's organizations move to new Bishop's Building
1911	Field Day replaces Annual Day and includes literature, music, and sports contests, held during June Conference
1912	Central board is renamed general board; first summer camp for girls is held (in Liberty Stake)
1913	Beehive Girls program is organized; first churchwide speech and other contests are held during June Conference
1914	Senior Girls program is divided into Seniors and Advanced Seniors; leadership week is instituted to train leaders; slogans are approved for girls to recite each year
1914–18	World War I
1918–45	Heber J. Grant, seventh president of Church
1920	YLMIA operates Beehive House as a home for girls; roadshows are put on by several stakes; Nineteenth Amendment to U.S. Constitution grants suffrage to women

1921   Intermediate Girls program is organized
            (renamed Junior Girls in 1922)

1922   Gold and green become official colors of MIA;
            first Gold and Green Ball is held; summer home
            for girls' camp is built at Brighton in canyon east
            of Salt Lake City

1923   MIA receives responsibility for entire Church
            recreation program

1924   Lessons are published in manuals; Senior Girls'
            name is changed to Gleaners

1925   Golden Jubilee is held with YMMIA

1926   Junior girls adopt rose as their class flower

1929   *Young Woman's Journal* is merged with
            Improvement Era; Great Depression begins

1929–37   RUTH MAY FOX serves as third president of Young
            Ladies' Mutual Improvement Association

1930   Church celebrates centennial; "Carry On" is
            written by Ruth May Fox for M-Men and Gleaner
            centennial celebration

1931   Lion House becomes social center for girls;
            cafeteria is opened in Lion House basement

1934   Name is changed to Young Women's Mutual
            Improvement Association (YWMIA)

1935   Scriptural themes replace slogans

1936   First MIA dance festival is held; Church welfare
            plan is inaugurated

1937   Gleaners adopt sheaf of wheat as symbol

1937–48   LUCY GRANT CANNON serves as fourth president of
            YWMIA

1939–45   World War II

1940   Golden Gleaner awards and Sunday evening
            firesides are introduced

1943   Junior class develops "Symbolism of the Rose"

1945–51   George Albert Smith, eighth president of Church

1946	Girls program is adopted by Presiding Bishopric (later transferred to YWMIA under Bertha S. Reeder)
1947	Centennial of pioneers' arrival in Salt Lake Valley
1948–61	BERTHA STONE REEDER serves as fifth president of YWMIA
1950	Age groups are realigned: Beehive Girls for ages 12–13, Mia Maids for ages 14–15, Junior Gleaners for ages 16–18, and Gleaners for ages 19–29; speech and quartet festivals are held in the field and at June Conference
1950–53	Korean War
1951–70	David O. McKay, ninth president of Church
1959–61	Beehive House is closed for restoration
1961–72	FLORENCE SMITH JACOBSEN serves as sixth president of YWMIA
1962	Worldwide youth conferences are held
1963–68	Lion House is closed for restoration
1965–73	Vietnam War
1967	MIA begins annual presentation of *Promised Valley*
1969	YWMIA observes centennial
1970–72	Joseph Fielding Smith, tenth president of Church
1971	*Ensign* replaces *Improvement Era* as magazine for adult members; *New Era* is published for youth
1972–73	Harold B. Lee, eleventh president of Church
1972	Name is changed to Aaronic Priesthood, Young Women
1972–78	RUTH HARDY FUNK serves as seventh president of Young Women
1973–85	Spencer W. Kimball, twelfth president of Church
1974	Name is changed to Young Women
1975	Last June Conference is held

1978   Revelation on priesthood; first general women's
              meeting broadcast

1978–84   ELAINE CANNON serves as eighth president of
              Young Women

1980   Sesquicentennial of Church; young women are
              encouraged to make banners representing
              commitment or heritage; consolidated meeting
              schedule begins, allowing Sunday instruction for
              young women; practice of repeating theme each
              week is reinstated

1984   Wives of international area presidencies begin
              serving as general board representatives for
              Relief Society, Young Women, and Primary;
              Relief Society and Young Women withdraw
              membership in National Council of Women and
              International Council of Women

1984–92   ARDETH GREENE KAPP serves as ninth president of
              Young Women

1985   At Young Women satellite broadcast, Young
              Women Values are introduced

1985   Ezra Taft Benson becomes thirteenth president
              of Church

1986   First worldwide Young Women celebration, with
              launching of balloons

1987   Age-group mission statements and Young
              Women logo are introduced

1988   Young Women, Relief Society, and Primary
              offices move into remodeled Relief Society
              Building

1989   Second worldwide Young Women celebration,
              with bell ringing

1990   Leadership guidebook is published

1991   Leadership video is released

1992   JANETTE CALLISTER HALES becomes tenth president
              of Young Women

1992	Third worldwide Young Women celebration, "Walk in the Light"
1993	New camp manual is introduced, with focus on service, spirituality, and the Young Women Values
1994	125th anniversary of Young Women

Notes

Introduction

1. *Times and Seasons*, April 1, 1843, 154, as quoted in "An Interesting Outgrowth of the Relief Society in Nauvoo," *Relief Society Magazine* 4 (March 1917): 123.

2. Ibid., 124.

3. Ibid., 126.

4. Ibid., 127.

5. Ibid., 128.

6. Marba C. Josephson, *History of the YWMIA* (Salt Lake City: Young Women's Mutual Improvement Association, 1955), 1–2.

7. "A Gathering Commitment to the Lord: A History of the Young Women" (Salt Lake City: The Church of Jesus Christ of Latter-day Saints, 1980).

Chapter One: Elmina Shepard Taylor

1. *A Century of Sisterhood: Chronological Collage, 1869–1969* (Salt Lake City: YWMIA, 1969), 38.

2. "Our Picture Gallery," *Young Woman's Journal* 2 (October 1890): 2–3.

3. "A Biographical Sketch of President Elmina S. Taylor," *Young Woman's Journal* 15 (January 1905): 3.

4. Susa Young Gates, *History of the Young Ladies' Mutual Improvement Association* (Salt Lake City: Deseret News, 1911), 90.

5. "Our Picture Gallery," 3.

6. Ibid.

7. Autobiography of George Hamilton Taylor (Privately published, 1949, in possession of Patricia J. Menlove), 11–12. Hereafter cited as George H. Taylor Autobiography.

8. Ibid.

9. "A Biographical Sketch," 5.

10. George H. Taylor Autobiography, 15.

11. Ibid., 16.

12. "Biographical Sketch of Mrs. Elmina S. Taylor, President of the YLMIA Associations," *Young Woman's Journal* 2 (October 1890): 3.

13. George H. Taylor Autobiography, 24–25.

14. Martha H. Tingey, "Past Three Score Years and Ten," *Young Woman's Journal* 12 (September 1901): 397–98.

15. George H. Taylor Autobiography, 35.

16. Ibid., 40.

17. Ibid., 45.

18. Ibid., 13–14.

19. Ibid., 47.

20. "Our Picture Gallery," 4.

21. Diary of Elmina Shepard Taylor, August 21, 1879, Church Archives.

22. Tingey, "Past Three Score Years and Ten," 397.

23. Diary of Elmina Shepard Taylor, June 30, 1879.

24. Quoted in Josephson, *History of the YWMIA*, 5–6 (reported June 19, 1900).

25. "A Gathering Commitment to the Lord: A History of Young Women," (Salt Lake City: The Church of Jesus Christ of Latter-day Saints, 1980).

26. Josephson, *History of the YWMIA*, 6.

27. *A Century of Sisterhood*, 23.

28. Gates, *History of the Young Ladies' Mutual Improvement Association*, 93–94.

29. Mae Taylor Nystrom, "The Y.L.M.I.A. under President Elmina S. Taylor," *Young Woman's Journal* 36 (June 1925): 330.

30. *A Century of Sisterhood*, 30–31.

31. Gates, *History of the Young Ladies' Mutual Improvement Association*, 181.

32. Ibid., 182.

33. "Our Picture Gallery," 4.

34. "Report of the Young Ladies' Mutual Improvement Associations of Utah," *Young Woman's Journal*, May 1891, 383.

35. "A Biographical Sketch," 6.

36. Blessing of Elmina S. Taylor, May 16, 1899, by Elder George Teasdale, Elmina S. Taylor Papers, Church Archives.

37. Josephson, *History of the YWMIA*, 13.

Chapter Two: Martha Horne Tingey

1. Thomas C. Romney, "Martha Horne Tingey," *Instructor*, July 1950, 198–99.

2. *Young Woman's Journal* 38 (October 1927): 625.

3. Emmeline B. Wells, "Martha Jane Horne Tingey," *Young Woman's Journal* 4 (January 1891): 147.

4. Ibid., 150.

5. Gates, *History of the Young Ladies' Mutual Improvement Association*, 287.

6. Arnold J. Irvine, "Martha Horne Tingey Directs Affairs of YLMIA for 24 Years," *Church News*, December 21, 1963, 16.

7. Interview with Burton and Joseph Tingey, January 31, 1991. Hereafter cited as Tingey Interview.

8. Family Group Sheet of Joseph and Martha Horne Tingey, Archives, LDS Family History Department.

9. Romney, "Martha Horne Tingey," 199.

10. Gates, *History of the Young Ladies' Mutual Improvement Association*, 288.

11. Ibid., 287.

12. Tingey Interview.

13. *A Century of Sisterhood*, 54.

14. Tingey Interview.

15. Gates, *History of the Young Ladies' Mutual Improvement Association*, 287.

16. Wells, "Martha Jane Horne Tingey," 152.

17. Ibid.

18. *Young Woman's Journal* 4 (1892–93): 549.

19. *A Century of Sisterhood*, 32.

20. Gates, *History of the Young Ladies' Mutual Improvement Association*, 95.

21. Ibid.

22. Ibid.

23. Romney, "Martha Horne Tingey," 199.

24. *A Century of Sisterhood*, 45.

25. Ibid., 46.

26. Ibid., 50.

27. *Young Woman's Journal*, 40 (May 1929): 311.

28. *A Century of Sisterhood*, 55.

29. Tingey Interview.

30. Ibid.

31. Ibid.

32. Ibid.

33. Ibid.

34. *Young Woman's Journal* 38 (October 1927): 636.

Chapter Three: Ruth May Fox

1. Ruth May Fox, "My Story," privately published, December 1973. Except as noted, all quotations are from this 91–page document, which is on file in the Church Archives.

2. Lucile C. Reading, "Ruth's Hikes," *Children's Friend,* November 1969, 23.

3. Letter of Vida Fox Clawson to Emily Clawson Wright, January 28, 1943, copy in possession of Janet Peterson.

4. Letter of Feramorz Y. Fox to Emily Clawson Wright, February 9, 1943, copy in possession of author, Janet Peterson.

5. Personal interview with Jean Cannon Willis, November 21, 1990.

6. Personal interview with George I. Cannon, November 21, 1990.

7. Elsie T. Brandley, "Ruth May Fox," *Young Woman's Journal* 40 (May 1929): 313.

Chapter Four: Lucy Grant Cannon

1. Interview with George I. Cannon, Jean Cannon Willis, and H. Stanley Cannon, November 21, 1990; hereafter cited as Cannon et al. Interview.

2. Ibid.

3. Mary Connelly Kimball, "Lucy Grant Cannon," *Young Woman's Journal* 34 (August 1923): 475.

4. Frances Grant Bennett, *Glimpses of a Mormon Family* (Salt Lake City: Deseret Book Company, 1968), 2.

5. Cannon et al. Interview.

6. Ibid.

7. Ronald W. Walker, "Heber J. Grant," in *Presidents of the Church,* ed. Leonard J. Arrington (Salt Lake City: Deseret Book, 1986), 235.

8. Marba C. Josephson, "Careers of Service to Young Womanhood," *Improvement Era* 40 (December 1937): 790.

9. Kimball, "Lucy Grant Cannon," 475.

10. Ibid., 476.

11. Copy of a letter from Heber J. Grant to Mr. and Mrs. O. L. Winters, dated March 21, 1912, following the death of their daughter. Original in the possession of Jean Cannon Willis.

12. Walker, "Heber J. Grant," 236.

13. Cannon et al. Interview.

14. Elsie Talmage Brandley, "Changes in the Presidency of the YWMIA," in Josephson, *History of the YWMIA,* 334.

15. Telephone interview with Jean Cannon Willis, December 6, 1990.

16. Cannon et al. Interview.

17. Interview with Florence Smith Jacobsen, October 15, 1990.

18. Telephone interview with Jean Cannon Willis, December 6, 1990.

19. Cannon et al. Interview.

20. Ibid.

21. Ibid.

22. Ibid.

23. Interview with Florence Smith Jacobsen, October 15, 1990.

24. Cannon et al. Interview.

25. Ibid.

26. Ibid.

27. Brandley, "Changes in the Presidency of the YWMIA," 333–34.

28. Ibid., 167–68.

29. Copy of letter written by Lucy Grant Cannon, dated January 18, 1934. Original in the possession of Jean Cannon Willis.

30. *A Century of Sisterhood,* 71.

31. Josephson, *History of the YWMIA,* 87.

32. Copy of Lucy Grant Cannon newsletter dated May 15, 1945. Original in the possession of Jean Cannon Willis.

33. Cannon et al. Interview.

34. Lucy Grant Cannon, "Experience," *Young Woman's Journal* 40 (August 1929): 410.

Chapter Five: Bertha Stone Reeder

1. "I Remember Sister Reeder," collection of tributes, in possession of Oertel Aadnesen Riley Hoit.

2. Ibid.

3. Diary of Bertha Julia Stone Reeder, in possession of Oertel Aadnesen Riley Hoit, n.d.

4. Bertha Stone Reeder Oral History, 1974, James H. Moyle Oral History Program, Church Archives, 2.

5. Telephone interview with Oertel A. Hoit, November 21, 1990.

6. Personal interview with Grant C. Aadnesen, November 19, 1990.

7. Telephone interview with Oertel A. Hoit.

8. Letter from Charles E. Peterson to Oertel A. Hoit, January 10, 1983.

9. Personal interview with Grant C. Aadnesen.

10. Telephone interview with Helena Larson Allen, November 15, 1990.

11. Telephone interview with Oertel A. Hoit.

12. Blessing given to Bertha S. Reeder, December 29, 1941, by President David O. McKay, Salt Lake City, Utah; copy in possession of Oertel A. Hoit.

13. Diary of Bertha Julia Stone Reeder.

14. Bertha Stone Reeder Oral History, 15.

15. Letter from Kenneth W. Porter to Oertel A. Hoit, December 31, 1982.

16. Bertha Stone Reeder Oral History, 8.

17. Ibid., 17.

18. Ibid., 7.

19. Diary of Bertha Julia Stone Reeder.

20. Ruth Hardy Funk Oral History, 1979, Church Archives, James Oral History Program, 31.

21. "If I Were in My Teens," *Improvement Era*, June 1954, 470.

22. Transcription of funeral service of Bertha Reeder Richards, December 30, 1982.

23. Bertha Stone Reeder Oral History, 41.

24. Ibid., 32.

25. As quoted by Verda Mae Christensen in telephone interview with author Janet Peterson, January 13, 1992.

26. Ibid.

27. Bertha Stone Reeder Oral History, 34.

28. Transcription of funeral service.

29. Ibid.

30. "I Remember Sister Reeder."

31. Diary of Bertha Julia Stone Reeder.

32. Bertha Stone Reeder Oral History, 9.

Chapter Six: Florence Smith Jacobsen

Note: Except as footnoted, all quotations and information are taken from interviews conducted with Florence S. Jacobsen by LaRene Gaunt on October 15 and December 6, 1990, and June 6, 1991, and a written statement by Florence Jacobsen, dated December 1990.

1. Dell Van Orden, " 'Woman of Conscience' Enjoys a Rich Heritage," *Church News*, December 14, 1968, 13.

2. Ibid.

3. Lavina Fielding, "Florence Smith Jacobsen: In Love with Excellence," *Ensign,* June 1977, 28.

4. Gerry Avant, "Historical Curator Is Appointed," *Church News,* June 9, 1973, 5.

5. Interview with Theodore C. Jacobsen, May 24, 1991.

6. Telephone interview with Theodore C. Jacobsen, June 10, 1991.

7. Interview with Theodore C. Jacobsen, May 24, 1991.

8. Ibid.

9. Florence S. Jacobsen, "Women, This Is Our Time," *Ensign*, March 1972, 39.

10. Telephone interview with Margaret R. Jackson Judd, June 6, 1991.

11. Telephone interview with Dorothy P. Holt, June 6, 1991.

12. Telephone interview with Helena W. Larson Allen, May 22, 1991.

13. "Missions in Europe Use MIA as Proselyting Tool," *Church News*, October 27, 1962, 13.

14. Telephone interview with Richard Oman, May 22, 1991.

15. "Woman of Conscience Award Presented," *Improvement Era*, December 1968, 112.

16. "Three Past MIA Leaders Honored at Reunion," *Church News*, June 23, 1973, 6.

17. Telephone interview with Richard Oman, May 21, 1991.

18. Avant, "Historical Curator Is Appointed."

19. Interview with Theodore C. Jacobsen, May 24, 1991.

Chapter Seven: Ruth Hardy Funk

Note: Except as footnoted, all quotations by Ruth Hardy Funk and details of her life are taken from Ruth Hardy Funk Oral History (1979, James H. Moyle Oral History Program, Church Archives), and from personal interviews with Ruth Hardy Funk, conducted by Janet Peterson, October 30, 1990, and May 15, 1991.

1. Jeane Woolfenden, "There's Always the Promise of Morning," *New Era*, May 1977, 29.

2. Bruce A. Van Orden, *Prisoner for Conscience' Sake: The Life of George Reynolds* (Salt Lake City: Deseret Book, 1992).

3. Telephone interview with Marcus C. Funk, January 8, 1991.

4. Telephone interview with Jennie Jo Funk Emery, May 16, 1991.

5. Ibid.

6. Telephone interview with Nancy Funk Pulsipher, May 17, 1991.

7. Ibid.

8. Telephone interview with Marcus C. Funk, January 8, 1991.

9. Telephone interview with Allyson Funk Gurney, January 8, 1991.

10. Telephone interview with Marcus C. Funk, January 8, 1991.

11. Telephone interview with Hortense Child Smith, January 9, 1991. (A widow, Hortense married Elder Eldred G. Smith, Patriarch to the Church, in 1978.)

12. Ibid.

13. Ardeth G. Kapp Oral History, James H. Moyle Church History Program, Church Archives, 84.

14. "The Aaronic Priesthood MIA," *Ensign*, July 1973, 80–81.

15. Ardeth G. Kapp Oral History, 90.

16. Quoted in ibid., 104.

17. Ibid., 107.

18. Ibid., 112–13.

19. Telephone interview with Hortense Child Smith, January 9, 1991.

20. Telephone interview with Nancy Funk Pulsipher, May 17, 1991.

Chapter Eight: Elaine Cannon

Note: Except as footnoted, all quotations by Elaine Cannon and details of her life are taken from Elaine Cannon Oral History (1979–1990, James H. Moyle Oral History Program, Church Archives), personal interviews with Elaine Cannon conducted by LaRene Gaunt on October 8 and December 12, 1990, and June 25, 1991; and a written statement of Elaine Cannon, dated July 1991.

1. Anthony J. Cannon, "A Tribute to Elaine Cannon." Copy in possession of LaRene Gaunt.

2. " 'Let Me Soar,' Women Counseled," *Church News*, October 17, 1981, 3.

3. Elaine Cannon, *The Summer of My Content* (Salt Lake City: Deseret Book, 1976), 61.

4. Minnie Egan Anderson, "Elaine Winifred Anderson Cannon," 1950. Copy in possession of author, LaRene Gaunt.

5. Cannon, *The Summer of My Content*, 8.

6. Interview with Tony Cannon, March 5, 1991.

7. Interview with D. James Cannon, April 16, 1991.

8. Interview with Tony Cannon, March 5, 1991.

9. Interview with James Q. Cannon, April 19, 1991.

10. Susan Cannon McOmber to LaRene Gaunt, June 1991.

11. Lynne Hollstein, "Preparation Began Early for New YW President," *Church News*, July 22, 1978, 4.

12. Ibid.

13. Interview with Tony Cannon, March 5, 1991.

14. Susan Cannon McOmber to LaRene Gaunt, June 1991.

15. Interview with Marion D. Hanks, March 8, 1991.

16. Interview with D. James Cannon, April 16, 1991.

17. Cannon, *The Summer of My Content*, 75–76.

18. Interview with Marion D. Hanks, March 8, 1991.

19. Elaine Cannon, *Life — One to a Customer* (Salt Lake City: Bookcraft, 1981), 93.

20. Interview with Winnifred Jardine, January 28, 1991.

21. Written statement from Holly Cannon Metcalf, July 9, 1991.

22. Elaine Cannon, *The Seasoning* (Salt Lake City: Bookcraft, 1981), 9.

23. Interview with James Q. Cannon, April 19, 1991.

24. Kathleen Lubeck, "On the Bright Side," *This People*, December 1982, 25.

25. Ibid.

26. Interview with Winnifred Jardine, March 8, 1991.

27. Written statement of Norma B. Smith, April 1991.

28. Cannon, *The Summer of My Content*, 75.

29. Interview with Laurel Bailey, January 25, 1991.

30. Hollstein, "Preparation Began Early for New YW President."

31. Interview with Marion D. Hanks, March 8, 1991.

32. Interview with James Q. Cannon, April 19, 1991.

33. "Aim Was Family Improvement," *Church News*, December 2, 1984, 10.

34. *This People*, March 1983, 55.

35. Ibid.

36. Elaine Cannon, "A Wonderful Adventure," *New Era*, April 1983, 12.

37. Elaine Cannon, "Reach for Joy," *Ensign*, May 1982, 95.

38. Interview with D. James Cannon, April 16, 1991.

39. Interview with Marion D. Hanks, March 8, 1991.

40. Written statement of Carla Cannon, March 1991.

41. Cannon, *Life — One to a Customer*, 94.

Chapter Nine: Ardeth Greene Kapp

Note: Except as footnoted, all quotations by Ardeth Greene Kapp are taken from Ardeth G. Kapp Oral History (James H. Moyle Oral History Program, Church Archives), and from an interview with Ardeth Greene Kapp, conducted by Janet Peterson on August 6, 1990.

1. Ardeth G. Kapp, "Stand Up, Lead Out," *New Era*, November 1985, 23.

2. Janet Peterson, "Friend to Friend," *Friend*, July 1985, 7.

3. Ibid.

4. Karen T. Arnesen, "Ardeth Greene Kapp: A Prairie Girl, A Young Woman Still," *Ensign*, September 1985, 36.

5. Peterson, "Friend to Friend," 6.

6. Ibid.

7. Ardeth G. Kapp, "Young Women Striving Together," *Ensign*, November 1984, 96–97.

8. Arnesen, "Ardeth Greene Kapp," 36.

9. Telephone interview with Heber B. Kapp, January 11, 1991.

10. Personal interview with Jayne B. Malan, May 22, 1991.

11. Telephone interview with Heber B. Kapp, January 11, 1991.

12. Arnesen, "Ardeth Greene Kapp," 37.

13. Ardeth G. Kapp, "Just the Two of Us — for Now," *Ensign*, February 1989, 21.

14. Ardeth G. Kapp, *My Neighbor, My Sister, My Friend* (Salt Lake City: Deseret Book, 1990), 127–28.

15. Kapp, "Just the Two of Us—for Now," 23.

16. Telephone interview with Shirley G. Burnham, January 10, 1991.

17. Telephone interview with Sharon G. Larsen, January 14, 1991.

18. Telephone interview with Shelly Larsen, January 19, 1991.

19. Arnesen, "Ardeth Greene Kapp,'" 38.

20. Written statement of Maurine J. Turley, May 31, 1991.

21. Personal interview with Patricia T. Holland, April 24, 1991.

22. Elaine L. Jack, "I Will Go and Do," *Ensign,* May 1990, 78.

23. Personal interview with Carolyn J. Rasmus, September 26, 1990.

24. Personal interview with Janette C. Hales, April 18, 1991.

25. Personal interview with Patricia T. Holland, April 14, 1991.

26. Personal interview with Jayne B. Malan, May 22, 1991.

Chapter Ten: Janette Callister Hales

Note: Except as footnoted, all quotations by Janette Hales and details of her life are taken from personal interviews conducted by Janet Peterson on April 8 and 20 and May 11, 1992, and a written statement of Janette Hales dated June 23, 1992.

1. Sheridan R. Sheffield, "Quest for Learning Is Her Trademark," *Church News,* April 18, 1992, 6.

2. "New Young Women General Presidency Called," *Ensign,* May 1992, 106.

3. Telephone interview with Jane Hales Ricks, May 12, 1992.

4. Telephone interview with Ann Hales Nevers, April 29, 1992.

5. Telephone interview with Jane Hales Ricks, May 12, 1992.

6. Telephone interview with Ann Hales Nevers, April 29, 1992.

7. Telephone interview with Karen Hales Parkinson, May 12, 1992.

8. Telephone interview with Jane Hales Ricks, May 12, 1992.

9. Written statement of Karol Gleave, May 5, 1992.

10. Telephone interview with Mary Hales, May 12, 1992.

11. Telephone interview with Ann Hales Nevers, April 29, 1992.

12. Telephone interview with Mary Alice Collins, May 11, 1992.

13. Telephone interview with Ann Edwards Cannon, May 21, 1992.

14. Telephone interview with Ann Hales Nevers, April 29, 1992.

15. Telephone interview with Thomas C. Hales, May 6, 1992.

16. Janette C. Hales, "You Are Not Alone," *Ensign,* May 1992, 79.

17. Telephone interview with Virginia H. Pearce, May 26, 1992.

18. Written statement of Ardeth G. Kapp, May 14, 1992.

19. Telephone interview with Mary Hales, May 12, 1992.

20. Personal interview with Carolyn J. Rasmus, May 14, 1992.

21. Telephone interview with Patricia P. Pinegar, May 19, 1992.

22. Ibid.
23. Telephone interview with Virginia H. Pearce, May 26, 1992.
24. Hales, "You Are Not Alone," 80.
25. Written statement of Ardeth G. Kapp, May 14, 1992.
26. Personal interview with Carolyn J. Rasmus, May 14, 1992.

Index